SIMPLICITY

kim thomas

FINDING

PEACE BY

UNCLUTTERING

YOUR LIFE

BROADMAN
& HOLMAN
PUBLISHERS

Nashville, Tennessee

0-8054-1853-9

Published by Broadman & Holman Publishers, Nashville, Tennessee
Acquisitions and Development Editor: Leonard G. Goss
Page Design and Typesetting: PerfecType

Dewey Decimal Classification: 248
Subject Heading: CHRISTIAN WOMEN
Library of Congress Card Catalog Number: 99-13531

Library of Congress Cataloging-in-Publication Data

Thomas, Kim. 1958-
    Simplicity : finding peace by uncluttering your life / by Kim
Thomas.
        p. cm.
    ISBN 0-8054-1853-9 (pbk.)
    1. Christian women—Religious life. 2. Simplicity—Religious
aspects—Christianity. I. Title.
    BV4527.T47   1999
    248.8'43—dc21

                                                    99-13531

                                                    CIP

DEDICATION

This book is dedicated to my family: my husband, my parents, my sister and her family, and all of the grandparents, aunts, uncles, cousins, in-laws, and dogs who have generously lived their lives in my presence. I love you.

"But I'm not joking. If my art played no part in my family's life, their lives and their achievements greatly influenced my art."

From *Self-Portrait* in Marc Chagall's series *My Life*, 1922

CONTENTS

INTRODUCTION:
THE NEED FOR
SIMPLICITY

When the toast is burning; you're late for work; your husband complains he has no clean socks; you drain the last of your total-coverage under-eye concealer on one eye; the sitter has called in sick for the day; you're down to one car because the minivan is in the shop being repaired after your son and his buddies used the tail pipe as a launchpad for a handful of bottle rockets; your single girlfriend has called in a state of panic because her flight to Paris for her ten-day getaway has been delayed two hours; your mother called to give you an update on your dad's state of mind after a forced early retirement; your daily devotion book has a bookmark on April 10 and today is September 1; the "Casserole Ministry" has left two messages on your machine wondering if you'll be delivering your tuna casserole with the potato chips on top to the church or directly to the Rogers' family because actually Allen Rogers is allergic to tuna and they need to switch your casserole with Sara Thompson's, which was going to the Marshal family, who just delivered their first child, and suddenly you realize you've locked yourself out of the house and have made nothing for your family for dinner and will have to call for pizza again, and you would shove your husband's hiking boots down Thoreau's throat if he even thought about talking to you about how he "went to the woods to live deliberately."

Somewhere along the road, the freedom to be wives, mothers, sisters, professionals, friends, and active women of God turned into an out-of-control steam engine aimed right at our self-worth. Freedom turned into obligation and pressure. We became guilty, fractured, and overwhelmed. Exhausted and defeated, we packed up our purses, diaper bags, briefcases, grocery bags, and suitcases and ran as fast as we could—all the while longing for peace and contentment and freedom from complexity or affectation. Now we hunger for ease, lack of hindrance, clarity, as well as definition and wholeness. Emerson spoke of it as "the sacredness of private integrity."

Simplicity.

It seems that the muchness, the manyness, and the busyness have caused us to trip over our lives, and we just hope to get to the end of the day in time to turn out the lights before the tenacious sun shows its face for another day.

Simplicity.

Through our bodies, we relate to our physical world, our environment. Through our souls, we relate to others and ourselves. And through our spirits, we relate to God. It is from this context of body, soul, and spirit that we will approach simplifying our lives.

There is good news. But the good news is not that there is a secret method or prayer to make all of the complexities of life go away. Nor is it that you have been granted a three-month monastic getaway where all of life will be understood by pondering a hazelnut, as Julian of Norwich did. However, the good news *is* that when we simplify our lives, we make more room for the image of God to be reflected in us. When this happens, we are closer to who he created us to be.

By simplifying our lives, we also create the opportunity to stop and listen long enough to reconnect with the One whose image we are to reflect and who speaks in a still small voice. Obviously this demands a bit of quiet to hear. Or at least the skill of interior quiet.

Simplicity.

THE PATTERN

I have been convinced for most of my life that there either was no pattern used to create me or that it was one with sketchy directions at best. I seem to have a distinct inability to "blend." This "differentness" honestly has no roots in political or social drives; I just always seem to choose the second or third most commonly accepted way to behave. I believe I exemplify the proverbial round-peg-square-hole syndrome. When I was younger, *weird* was the word. Now that I am fully grown, it's been sensitively softened to *eccentric*.

In this era of self-examination, I have probed the recesses of my childhood memories and come up with no traumatic incident on which to put the blame. It seems I just came this way. The proof is in the photos.

My sister was born first, and she used up all our family's pretty baby genes. Her baby pictures are like angels captured in black and white. Mine are more like angels past their curfews. She had that perfect little curl on her forehead, a gently upturned nose, and cherub-like lips that said rose-red, even in black and white.

My baby photos begin with hair: a massive gathering of thick black hair, each hair pursuing a different direction, so there was no way for it to be coaxed into a cooperative feminine statement. The nurses in the delivery room did their best to coif me, but even with the assistance of gel, spit, and Vaseline, the closest thing they could develop was an upswept Mohawk effect with a bit of a fold at the top. Now having tamed the beast of my hair, they were faced with the next challenge involved in those "welcome to the planet" baby pictures: how to hold up my head.

Realizing that I was barely born and rather busy with new things like breathing, they decided to prop me up on my little elbows. Fine move, technically speaking, but the results were not rewarded. Below my crown of black beauty was a face with a large concentration of body fat. My two tiny fists disappeared into the mounds of face-flesh, forcing my eyes into little beady brown slits, looking out over an open, toothless mouth.

I think you can clearly see the seeds of an unusual woman in the making. Much to my disappointment, this weirdness was not a condition I could expect to outgrow. I was a Camp Fire Girl when everyone else was a Girl Scout. I was short, but I was a high-scoring guard on the basketball team. I was a math major who switched to art, a blonde who colors her hair black, and, to top it all off, I am a caffeine-free vegetarian in a happy childless marriage. My weirdness is no longer as much about my appearance, but more about "social blending," or fitting in.

While I have spent much of my life feeling like I don't fit in, I am reminded that I was "fearfully and wonderfully made"(Ps. 139). I am intentionally designed and a perfect fit for my skin. It doesn't change the quirks or flaws; it just makes them OK.

Genesis 1:26–28 speaks of God creating male and female in his image. *Imago Dei.* The Hebrew word used for image here is *tselem,* derived from the root word meaning to cut, or carve. It is said that when Michelangelo was asked how he created such beautiful sculptures, he replied, "I just cut away everything that doesn't look like the image I'm trying to create."

It's been a long time and many miles since the garden, so we may have some cutting away to do to reflect more accurately the image of God. This is where simplicity becomes the right tool for the job.

When we sew, we use a pattern and cut away everything that doesn't look like the item we are making. The pattern makes the going a little easier. It is like that in our lives, too. As we look at *Simplicity: A Life Patterned After God,* we will discover how to (1) reduce the clutter, (2) persevere in the everyday, and (3) focus on the goal. We find this pattern in Hebrews 12:1–2: "Let us . . . lay aside every encumbrance, and the sin which so easily entangles us [this is the reducing-the-clutter part], and let us run with endurance the race that is set before us [this is the persevering part], fixing our eyes on Jesus, the author and perfecter of faith [this is the focusing part]" (NASB). Applying the pattern to our physical world, emotional world, and spiritual world (or body, soul, and spirit) will lead us down the path of simplicity.

PART I.

BODY:
SIMPLICITY
IN OUR
PHYSICAL WORLD

"The world is a net; the more we stir in it, the
more we are entangled."
—Anonymous

"We know that you've got treasure here," the
leader says. "If you won't show us where it's hid,
we'll beat you till you tell." . . .
"Did they but know," I say, "the only treasure
old men have lies buried deep in graves."
—Frederick Buechner

Here is a 1990s version of a beautiful passage of Scripture. I imagine it would go something like this:

"Now as they were traveling along, he entered a certain village; and a woman named Martha welcomed him into her home. And she had a sister called Mary who moreover was listening to the Lord's word, seated at his feet. But Martha was distracted because the place-card holders made out of tiny apples with votives and little cards sliced into them, and the centerpiece made by hammering holes in a tin can, threading twine or ribbon through the holes for a handle, knotting it and filling it with fresh posies and anemones, hand rolled beeswax candles, delightful pear tarts and many other GOOD THINGS were not ready yet, so she came to him and said, 'Lord, do you not care that my sister Mary Stewart has left me to do all the serving alone? Then tell her to help me.' But the Lord answered and said to her, 'Martha, Martha, you are worried and bothered about so many things: but only a few things are necessary, really only one, for Mary has chosen the REALLY GOOD THING, which shall not be taken away from her'" (Luke 10:38–42).

Before we go any further, let me make a mild disclaimer for the Marthas here. In Bible times and culture, the roles for women were strictly defined and primarily limited to domestically oriented functions. Jesus came along and revolutionized life for women by allowing them to be included in educational settings and to choose to pursue spiritual things. So Martha was just following tradition, and she was a little slower than Mary at receiving the emancipation Jesus had brought.

And then there's Martha Stewart. While making some of us a little crazy at our ineptness at tying bows, she has made it domestically correct to grab a handful of wildflowers from the backyard, toss them in an empty pickle jar, tie some twine around it, and throw it ever so casually on the table as a centerpiece. This in place of the lead crystal vase full of expensive long-stem roses required in the past. She has made *simple chic* vogue.

As we seek to reflect the image of God more accurately, we will begin by simplifying our physical world. And when I speak of the body, or the physical world, I'm not talking about the physiological functions of these flesh-and-blood housings. Thanks to divine design, our bodily systems tend to function without our having to direct them. Our respiratory, circulatory, digestive, and sensory systems need little coaxing, except in cases of illness or trauma, to do what they were intended to do. Recognizing that we could discuss eating habits, exercise, and other subjects relating to our physical body, I'd like to direct our thoughts more toward our physical world as it pertains to our living environment.

This seems a reasonable place to start because we can see and touch it. As we begin to develop skills of simplicity, actually seeing what can be simplified as we relate to our physical world will make it easier to approach our interior world. When our physical world spirals out of control and our lists of lists no longer seem remotely useful, it is good to remember the message of Ecclesiastes 3. There is a time for everything (and my mother would add and "a place"), and a season for every delight under heaven.

Martha was clearly overwhelmed with the things, the tasks, and the shortage of time needed to accomplish her goals as they related to her physical world. Because we often run at this same feverish pitch, we need to implement some practical nuts-and-bolts cleverness if we are indeed to simplify our lives while we hold on to this spinning planet beneath our feet.

1

REDUCING THE CLUTTER

What is so seductive about a full attic? Or so irresistible about a full basement? Or so mesmerizing about a packed closet or drawers that bust forth? I remember as a girl being totally uninterested in my mother's dresser drawers. It was probably due to her instinctive gift of "de-clutter." In one drawer there would be four neatly folded pairs of "functioning" pantyhose (purposely separated from the trouser hose, the ones with runs in them), seven identical pairs of panties folded in thirds and then halves, three bras folded cup-in-cup, and a flowery-smelling sachet in the midst of this neatness. This was representative of her other drawers. Don't get me going on her linen closet.

There was absolutely no mystery to be discovered in those drawers. All the items in them were full-fledged members of her wardrobe, so there were no surprises, nothing I hadn't seen before. On the other hand, Mom did allow for three small indulgences in the "stuff I never use but still save" category: the attic, Dad's jewelry box, and the out-of-date-clothes basket.

Even on the hottest day in the summer, I could entertain myself with the mysteries of the attic. My old toys and stuffed animals, my older sister's old toys and stuffed animals, and exotic items from Dad's many tours to places like the South Pole and the Orient held me long after the sweating began.

The wonder that was created by boxes labeled simply "Books" sent me into hyperimagination. If the attic was entirely too hot and unbearable, a pass through Dad's jewelry box with the many bejeweled cufflinks and tie bars, old unworn rings, and multicolored ribbons symbolizing honors earned in service to his country would capture me for an afternoon. And the out-of-date-clothes basket, which at the time seemed so big and heavy, would net me many in a long line of one-of-a-kind fashions.

While I maintained a cache of baby dolls so large that my friends and I often played "Adoption," Mom's gift for de-cluttering was forced on her early due to my father's career in the Navy. Every eighteen months to two years we would be notified of our new geographical location. Moving a home of four (not counting the baby dolls) so often can keep a girl lean on the "stuff" side of life. I think we probably had just enough clutter to keep my youthful creative juices flowing, but not enough to choke on.

So why do we have full attics, basements, closets, and drawers? I'm sure somewhere there is a psychologist who would rationalize it as having something to do with thumb sucking, but I think it has more to do with making a statement of permanency and ownership of our place on this planet. However, maintaining the eternal perspective that this world is not our home and that everything we have is a gift from God will help push us toward detaching from "things."

My theory is that we will fill whatever space we are allotted. We moved from an "efficient" (whoever named it that has obviously never lived in one) one-thousand-square-foot apartment to our two-thousand-square-foot home. The first thing I did was go into each room, fully extend my arms, and do an impromptu little dance. I'm not a very gifted dancer, but I just wanted to feel the space. We were so overcrowded in our womb-like apartment that our home felt like a warehouse . . . just waiting to be filled.

I was recently reminded of how pristine and huge our basement was back then. I was looking for the leftover paint for the exterior of our house to do some touch-up. After rummaging through a convicting amount of stuff, I found a can and proceeded with my task. The next day, I went out to inspect my now-dry work, only to discover that I had used the wrong can of paint. By sundown the next day, I found myself in the presence of a leaned, cleaned, and weaned basement.

Many times my husband and I have spent an evening in our home watching a rented movie. By the end of the evening, our two miniature schnauzers have collected their most favored toys and brought them all into the room. It's as if they are saying, "You're here, we're here, our stuff is here. We're not leaving." I recently stacked their two dog beds in the hall for delivery to the basement, since they haven't slept in them in months. I came down the hallway only to discover Rose, the sentimental one, lying in her bed. I could almost hear her saying, "I know I never use it, but it's mine."

A friend sat in our den with us recently lamenting the fact that he had to go empty out a storage unit he was renting. He was trying to reduce his outgoing expenses, and the $200-a-month rental "box" was a good start. We were shocked to know he still had a storage unit, as he and his family had moved into a three-thousand-plus-square-foot house, and he was maintaining a twelve-hundred-square-foot office space. We had helped him empty another storage unit the year before. We began to discuss some of the items in this unit, and it was instantly clear to me that he was a prime candidate for simplifying his life. He had caseload boxes of stuff from each of his many successful entrepreneurial ventures and more unusable stuff than I had seen in my lifetime. He was in a transitional time in his life, waiting on the Lord for career direction, and it seemed that these things symbolized a time of comfort and success. But they also were an anchor around his soul, keeping him from detaching from things as well as the past. At the end of the evening, he had committed to the "stuff-reduction act" and gave me a smirk as he said, "Well, Kim, there's a little story for your book, hmmm?"

Perhaps a healthy combination of conviction and inconvenience can lead us to our need for simplicity. Thomas Merton said, "It gives great glory to God for a person to live in this world using and appreciating the good things of life without care, without anxiety, and without inordinate passion."[1] In many ways, to hold things loosely, to need them, but need them not. To have them, but not *need* to have them. He summarized this thought by saying, "We cannot use created things without anxiety unless we are detached from them." There is no better way to begin to detach from things than to lean, clean, wean, and begin to organize the "things" in our lives.

While I have never appeared on one of those morning shows with a hundred ways to organize your life, I have studied under the tutelage of my mom, and I think that qualifies me to give some suggestions. Here are a few.

CLOTHES CLOSETS

Let's start with an obvious one. If someone knocked at your door right now, would you run in a panic to be sure your closet doors were all closed? Or would you, with gladness of heart, sashay to the door in confidence that all of your closets are color organized and that their floors have only enough shoes to be worn in one week? As we consider reducing the clutter in order to simplify our lives, a seasonal look into our clothes closets is necessary.

The fashion industry sets us up for full closets by changing trends so often. In turn, we fall victim to the industry when we allow ourselves to be defined by what we wear instead of who we are. Mary Kay Ash, the cosmetics entrepreneur, said that because women don't know how great they are, they "come to us all vogue outside and vague inside." Her wisdom is reminiscent of God's reminder to Samuel when he was finding the next king for God to anoint. In 1 Samuel 16:7, God reminded him that while man may look at the outward appearance, God looks at the inward condition of the heart.

While clothing is a necessity, clothing should never outshine or outshout who we are inside.

As we consider the practical nuts and bolts of cleaning our closets, let us lead with the inside, and let our sense of style be determined by who we are rather than the "styles" or trends of our time. This way, we don't become victims, but instead advocates of sensible thinking. It doesn't rule out the occasional radical orange sweater with red berries on it that doesn't go with anything, but it is a reasonable reckoning with the urge to have and the freedom not to.

I've been known to don a radical rag or two in my day, particularly when I was scouring the thrift stores. However, one day I approached my closet in such fashion exhaustion that I made a pact to limit my selections. If there was anything in my closet that didn't look good on me, even on my best days, I discarded it. If I hadn't worn it once that season, I tossed it. If it didn't support who I wanted to project from the inside, I lost it. I began to carefully wean myself of any clothes that I would be physically uncomfortable wearing. You know, the collection of "If I only wear it for a couple of hours, I can still breathe" stuff. If it looked great, but creeped, crawled, or constrained, it was still out. And then I packaged the retiring garments in a bundle bag and grinned at the thought of someone rejoicing at coming upon one of my treasures in a thrift store.

The danger here is that upon creating space in our closets, we feel that instinctive urge to fill them up again. Upon pondering your next purchase, you might want to consider three things: (1) if it doesn't add something essential, resist it; (2) if it doesn't look great, or feel great, just say no; and (3) if you have to do complicated logarithms to justify how expensive it is, do the sensible thing and turn your back and run. Simply put, it should be functional, flattering, and fiscally sound.

It is amazing the freedom that comes in reducing the choices. I can get dressed pretty quickly now because I know that anything I grab out of the closet has been scrutinized for its flatter-ability and comfort. While extreme formulas for wardrobe selection based on things like your colors, seasons, fruits, and alphabetical personality types can be irritatingly obsessive, a seasonal inventory of usable and unusable clothes, shoes, and accessories will give you a lot of mental and physical space to use elsewhere.

HOUSEHOLD GOODIES

Once you finish going through your clothes closets, your next step is to rid yourself of those household items you don't need. Keep the goal in mind: "We want to *reduce the clutter.*" Consider the bowling pin he had in the living room when you got married, the spitting fish vase you got from Aunt Ruth, the paperback books you've already read, the cabinets full of Tupperware that is unburpable because the lids to the containers have run away with the missing socks from the dryer. Then free yourself of these things. Have a yard sale.

One summer our income was unexpectedly and drastically reduced. We gathered up the unusable "junk and stuff" from our closets, cabinets, basement, and any other visible hiding places. We put them on tables or scattered them around the yard, and by the end of the second day, we had two months' rent in cash.

The first time I did a yard sale, I defeated the entire purpose of simplifying my life. I bought a ledger book, wrote in every item, including the iron with the missing plug and the assembled bouquet of hair ribbons. Then I put a sticker with an identifying letter code on each item, and as something sold, I recorded it in the ledger book.

There are many ways of managing a simple yard sale. You can group items of like price. For example, anything in this box is fifty cents, any shirt two dollars, items on this table five dollars each. Or you can make up prices as you go, although as a frequent yard sale attendee, I don't vote for this method. And my favorite idea is the way my sister does a yard sale. She puts out lunch bags, grocery bags, and leaf bags and prices them accordingly. Anything you can get in the lunch bag is three dollars, anything in the grocery bag ten dollars, and anything in the leaf bag twenty-five dollars. You have to have the mind-set starting out that anything that doesn't sell does not come back into your home. That leads us to another alternative for purging yourself of unneeded household items: charities.

Call Goodwill, Salvation Army, or any other local charity for a pickup. We have organizations in town that will even come at the end of the day and take everything that didn't sell at a yard sale. This is a wonderful service and gives you no excuse not to get rid of that recliner in need of a new home or the bicycle you've ridden once this decade, or curtains that don't match any room in your house any more. The tax-deductible receipt is sometimes more valuable than the time and effort involved in a yard sale, and your donation can help meet someone else's needs.

Consider donating books and magazines to a local nursing home. Take CDs, cassettes, and even records to the local used music store and sell them. We even discovered a consignment furniture store that would come to our house and give us estimated prices for saleable items and then haul them to the store. We sold a television, entertainment center, and a set of bookshelves through them. We simplified our lives and made what we call "free" money.

My grandmother on my dad's side was a classic pack rat. When paper towels were on sale, she would buy a case. That was fine, except she would store them upstairs and forget they were there, until she went upstairs to store the ten extra copies of the new Billy Graham book (well, they were new a couple of years ago, but a dollar apiece at the thrift store was too good to pass up). We had jokes in our family about her comical eccentricity. I have a picture of myself sitting in a chair in my grandparents' spare bedroom on Cape Cod, wearing three hats, holding four pocketbooks. All of these items had to be removed from our bed so we could get in it. I admired some candleholders in their house on that same trip and my granddad said to take them home with me. My grandmother, not wanting me to get something without my sister getting something as well, asked what I thought she might enjoy. I seized on the opportunity to let my sister know I was thinking of her, far away in Texas where she lived, and I impishly suggested that she would very much appreciate the set of plastic swans with plastic blue roses in them. UPS will deliver just about anything.

When you endeavor to rid yourself of household goodies, ask yourself, "Have I used it this past year?" If not, let it go. I guarantee you the reduction will free you. So what about those truly one-of-a-kind misfits cluttering your house? Wrap that spitting fish vase and give it to a depressed friend. You know Aunt Ruth would want it that way.

CHRISTMAS DECORATIONS

I am a Christmas fanatic. Around August I'm ready to start slowly introducing the Bing Crosby Christmas CD into our listening routine. It is all I can do to wait until Thanksgiving to set up a Christmas tree. And even then, it isn't just one Christmas tree, but four. And that's when I'm using self-control.

Some people would look on with admiration at my Christmas decorating zeal, while others would look on and encourage me to get a life. Still other dear friends and family consider it a highly serious neurosis.

It all sort of snuck up on me. We were traveling so much that my sensibilities said, "Let's get a fake tree, so as to minimize fire hazards." Now in its innocent beginning, this was an attempt at simplifying. Purchasing the perfectly shaped, short-needled, crayon-green tree was supposed to make quick work of my Christmas decorating. I hung on each twisted wire branch the few ornaments we had collected as well as the many dough ornaments I had lovingly made over the years. I was content. That lasted for one year.

The next year, I came across an irresistible find. (Please keep in mind that words like irresistible were in my vocabulary before I began simplifying my life.) I discovered a perfectly intact archaeological find from the '50s—a silver foil tree complete with rotating colored spotlight. I snatched my find up and hurried to the checkout counter of the downtown Salvation Army Thrift Store and counted out twelve one-dollar bills. By the end of that night I had made, baked, and painted thirty-eight "rein-steers" to hang on my tree. "Rein-steers" were my attempt at a southern Christmas. They were cattle with reindeer antlers that hung precariously on the Christmas tree. My family and friends began to look up *neurosis* in their home health guides.

As the following Christmas season approached, everything was over-shadowed by the death of my grandmother. I attended her funeral in Hyannis, Massachusetts, a couple of days before Thanksgiving. I attribute my purchase of a solid white tree decorated in antique ornaments from the thirties and forties to my nostalgia for my grandmother. The five-foot fluffy white tree with delicate painted and fading ornaments was a reminder of my grandmother with the fluffy white hair and delicate fading body that year.

The next season, I went fairly inconspicuous with my purchase of a table-top two-and-a-half-foot tree, one twelve-inch tree, one antique three-foot scraggly excuse for a tree, and one Martha-Stewart-looking tree to put on the mantle. I decorated each by taking apart several sizes of fake fruit grapes in "theme" colors and quietly whistled "O Tannenbaum" to myself.

It was clear the next year, as my husband and I were making the necessary repeated trips up and down the basement stairs, carrying a variety of boxes in various stages of "tatterous-ness," that when I suggested I would like to add a real Douglas fir tree to the decorating festivities, that something must be done to tame the beast that had gestated in me. I must digress a little here and remind you of my context, or family history.

Every year we had a family conflict of whether to icicle or not to icicle the tree. With my father in favor and my mother opposed, a small tit-for-tat tradition was devised. My father insisted that the icicles be placed one at a time on the tree, equally distributed to please a naval officer's eye for detail. In retaliation, my mother insisted that when we took down the tree, those same icicles be removed one at a time and returned to their box for next year. For years my peacemaker's heart would not take sides, but in adolescence, I began to voice my displeasure with the entire icicle controversy. That year we came upon the Tinsel-Détente Accord. We opted for tacky garland.

With this as my background, I began to search for compromises and simplification in my holiday routine. My family and friends rejoiced. Here are some things I found helpful:

If storage space allows, the most wonderful convenience of all is to store your trees fully decorated. Many stores sell Christmas tree bags, and if you can't find them, a large trash bag and twist-tie substitute perfectly.

I don't have that kind of storage space, except in the case of the smaller trees, so I opted for a collection of what I call "tree-coffins" (not a very festive title, but descriptive). I purchased large plastic crates that will hold one dismantled tree each. One box was just a couple of inches short, so I cut a small hole to accommodate the large piece. They stack on each other perfectly and keep out moisture and basement bugs. A small piece of masking tape identifies the contents, and that was that.

For the many varieties of ornaments, I purchased smaller storage boxes and grouped the ornaments in themes and colors. Once again using the hi-tech device of masking tape and pen, I labeled them. The rein-steers met up with an unfortunate "accident" when my husband knocked the silver tree over one year. But all the other ornaments are surviving their three-season sleep safely and simply in the basement.

SIMPLE SUMMARY

As we begin to detach from "things," we begin to conform to the pattern, to "lay aside every encumbrance" (Heb. 12:1, NASB). While things themselves are a-spiritual, meaning they are in themselves neither spiritual nor unspiritual, our attachment to them is a matter for personal reflection.

Mies van der Rohe, the German architect, became famous for his strong but simple architecture. His steel and glass structures, located at 860–880 Lake Shore Drive in Chicago, became the icon of city architecture for the mid-twentieth century. His buildings speak to the philosophy of style he became known for, when he said, "Less is more." Maintaining this same attitude when it comes to collecting things here in our physical world will lead us to a philosophy of life found in Matthew 6:19. Our treasures on earth should be *less* so that our treasures in heaven can be *more*. Because where our treasure is, that's where our heart will be. Our earthly collections are subject to the decay process of this natural world and will eventually break and fall apart and hold no value.

Even our bodies, those most amazing creations of blood, skin, and bone personally stained with the breath of God, will someday break down and function no more. Being aware of this, how can we carry on such attachment to the so-much-lesser "things" of creation? While the average life span of an American is eighty years, I can leave my charming fat-tire bicycle to which I am so attached out on the back porch over a rainy weekend and see signs of rust begin to form immediately. In the span of one summer's storage, I can lose treasured sweaters from the '40s and one-of-a-kind Pendleton wool shirts to an average family of moth larvae. The earthly baubles and treasures that are so vulnerable to the destruction of this world must never collect in such a pile that our vision of Christ is blocked or strained.

As a young preteen, I adopted a habit, popular at the time, of putting stickers, photos, and other treasures on my mirror. The idea was that as I got dressed and combed my hair I would see them and be reminded of special things. This innocent hobby began to lose its charm when I filled my mirror so full that my own image became blocked.

As we try to simplify our lives by reducing the clutter in our physical world and in our bodies, let me remind us that the ultimate goal is to more clearly reflect the image of God. When our lives become so full of things, we can easily block the image we were meant to reflect, as well as make it difficult for us to "fix our eyes on Jesus."

Obviously, this is in no way an exhaustive look at reducing our clutter and finding efficient ways of storing the things we have. But it is a jump start that pushes us toward enjoying the things we have instead of being consumed with acquiring. In the flurry of cleaning out you will be surprised to become reacquainted with old "friends." The teapot that you used every morning one fall after you sent your child off to her first year of school was lost behind other unused kitchen nonsense. Now you are ready to reintroduce it to your life. And you discover in the overall process that you have some very beloved treasures that make your home *your* home.

2

PERSEVERING IN THE EVERYDAY

It is my guess that whoever came up with the derogatory stereotype of a housewife sitting around in a chiffon dress eating bonbons and watching television never cleaned a toilet. Tasks that invoke moans and moments of depression are not often accompanied by glamour and great snacks.

I remember my father trying to help me maintain a positive attitude while I performed typical childhood chores by engaging me in a rousing aria of "Whistle While You Work," following it up with the cheerful "Heigh-ho, Heigh-ho, It's Off to Work We Go." As I pictured the Disney dwarfs happily working, I busily proceeded with my work as well. Not only was my father the impresario of sleight-of-hand and distraction concerning unpleasant chores, but my mother became a legend to my sister and me for being able to "make a party out of a can of black-eyed peas."

When faced with the mundane or the less than favorable, my mother would be at her best. Impulsive road trips to see family were one of her specialties. Because my father was in the Navy, he was stationed on ships and away from home often. Therefore, I have many a memory of last-minute late-night trips near holidays. One Christmas Eve, she decided that we three girls needed to be with family. With a sleepy joy, I was allowed to ride the new tricycle Santa delivered a few hours early, and then was swept away in footed pajamas only to wake up at my cousins' house, an easy hour-and-a-half flight away. That spontaneous decision transformed a meager Christmas into a joyfully perseverable family reunion.

Other family road trips were within driving distance. We made quick work of the travel by playing car games we invented. We also got pretty good at singing our favorite car songs like "Whispering Hope" and "Michael Row the Boat Ashore," with sister Melani on the ukulele. I even read my first word on one of our trips home: "M-e-m-p . . . Memphis!"

The source of Mother's fame came from her ability to charm us with a dinner of black-eyed peas and cornbread. When funds were low and Mom was blue, out would come the can. In her gifted way of silly fun and enthusiasm, an everyday experience became a tradition and symbol of the solidarity and camaraderie between a mother and her teenage and grade-school daughters.

Mom came by her gift naturally. All the women in her family—six sisters plus my grandmother—had it. The eldest of the sisters, my Aunt Mary, had enjoyed a wonderful long marriage to a loving husband when it was discovered that he had Parkinson's disease. She cared for him at home as long as possible, until he needed to be in a maximum care facility. She spent long hours sitting and just being with him there. She also knew how to persevere in the everyday. Every afternoon she would put on her brightly colored nylon jogging suit and awkward, large white jogging shoes, put my uncle in a wheel chair, and take off around the corridors of the nursing home. My husband and I thought the mobile party could be enhanced so we sent a boom box with an assortment of "music to persevere by."

My mother, the youngest of the six sisters, learned from my aunt about persevering. It continued through the bloodline to my sister's daughter. When my niece was four years old, my sister was in a near-fatal car accident. The accident was in February, and by Easter she was out of the critical care unit and in her own private room. We dressed my young niece in a perfect pale blue Easter outfit, with dress, jacket, gloves, lace socks, and hat. We were hoping to cheer up my sister by bringing her daughter by the hospital after church so she could see her all dressed up. The plan was more than slightly foiled when my niece ran into an aggressive pint of chocolate milk in children's church. As we carried her up in the elevator, dark brown stains covering her dress, jacket, and socks, she reminded us how to persevere in the face of spills. "I didn't get any chocolate milk on my hat!" she said with a smile that showed all of her tiny little teeth. And we began to persevere.

Because life is filled with chores, holiday-pressures, people who need you, and, of course, the proverbial spilt milk, we must learn to persevere in the everyday. We will look at some practical suggestions to make this easier, but it is the mind-set behind functioning in the everyday that needs to undergird all our efforts. Two thoughts will help equip us to persevere.

First, even if we are efficient in our everyday schedules, we can fall into the trap of enduring rather than persevering. Enduring is more along the lines of tolerating, or putting up with. And, in fact, the word itself is derived from the Latin *indurare,* meaning "to harden the heart." It would be very easy to develop a hard heart if our daily existence became about tolerating. On the other hand, persevering carries with it the notion of holding steadfast to a purpose, with a goal in mind. And, in fact, we are promised in Romans 5:4 that perseverance will bring about character.

The second thought is found in Philippians 4:11, 13. Paul spoke confidently when he said, "I have learned to be content in whatever circumstances . . . I can do all things through Him who strengthens me"(NASB). As we consider some practical ways to persevere in the everyday, this paradigm will serve us well. Finding joy in the faithfulness to life's everydayness leads us to the doorstep of contentment.

Most of life is composed of everyday, mundane tasks and experiences, and the sooner we begin to persevere instead of endure, to find contentment in all things, the sooner the ordinary is transformed into the extraordinary.

We begin to see the person on the other side of the need, the opportunity that persevering gives for developing character, and the contentment found in daily faithfulness made possible by the strength of the One who made us. And, ironically, the complex is made simple.

CHORES

My husband defines an essential as that which must be, so that that which may be, may be. Chores are essentials. Clothes must be cleaned so that those who need to wear clothes may wear clothes. Taxes must be prepared so that those who pay taxes may pay taxes. Lawns must be mowed so that life in suburbia may go on. Are you catching the rhythm here?

In 1990, the average woman spent forty-two fewer hours per week on housework than she did in 1900. By 1960, more than 96 percent of American households had electric refrigerators, which reduced shopping frequency and provided for time-saving leftovers. By 1990, 73 percent of American families had automatic washing machines, compared with the almost universal use of the washboard in 1900. In 1900, very few homes had cold running water, but by 1990, 98 percent had both hot and cold running water.[1] Life has definitely improved for the domestic technician, but because the efficient survival of the average American family is quite dependent on everyday types of chores, I would like to suggest three ways to simplify persevering in them: (1) make it fun, (2) consolidate, and (3) delegate.

I started to suggest that the most helpful first step is to hire a housecleaner. But aside from the fact that you have to clean house before the person comes and that it can be financially indebting, it also takes away a soul connection between you and your home. We tried having someone come clean once a month for about a year, and it was freeing in a sense. But I began to miss the alliance created between me and my nest when I was scrubbing floors, sinks, tubs, and toilets. I missed intimately knowing all of the flaws and charming personality marks of my home. But to net this joy and keep up with all of the other things in our lives, we really had to simplify.

Make it fun. Doctors have long touted laughter as a healer and stress reducer. Our ability to laugh and enjoy the everyday chores in our lives will turn them from humdrum responsibilities into play. So, vacuum naked. Scrub floors to your favorite CD at top volume. Clean the shower while you're in it and rinse it by spitting water. Make putting away his ten thousand socks into a basketball game by tossing them into his drawer from across the room. Serve frozen dinners by candlelight. Do the week's ironing while you watch a video you wanted to see. Put intimate notes in your husband's suit pockets when you pick them up from the dry cleaners. When your children don't put away their things, put them (the things) into the "black hole" box for a week's prison sentence. Give yourself rewards for balancing the checkbook or paying the bills, like a frozen Coke in a small six-and-a-half-ounce bottle or two fistfuls of M&Ms. When you are running Mom's Taxi Service, demand a tip in the form of your children telling you something they are grateful for every time they get out of the car. Bathe the pet and the children in the same tub at the same time. Plan your nervous breakdowns to fall on weekends. And, all in all, rejoice in the fact that you can buy a size smaller pants after having worked your rear end off. The laughter you generate will fuel your soul.

Consolidate. This entails thinking about what needs to be done in advance. Here are some ways to do it: Run errands to the same part of town together. Pay the bills and balance the checkbook in the same sitting. Grocery shop in one of those stores that has a dry cleaner, bank, drugstore, pharmacy, optical center, post office, and oil change center. Once you have the mop and bucket out, mop all the floors at one time. Clean sinks, tubs, and toilets on Mondays. Do laundry once a week instead of any time something is dirty. Clean out the refrigerator the night before trash day so it doesn't fill up the garbage for a week. Clean the windows in one room each Saturday in the spring until they have all been done. When making food for a friend, make a double recipe so your dinner is made, too. Use soap with a moisturizer in it, toothpaste with a whitener in it, and shampoo with a conditioner in it. I have a friend who has a friend who even does stomach crunches while she flosses. No one wants a strict boot-camp type of regimen, but an eye to consolidating will buy seconds that add up to minutes and hours of that most precious of commodities: time.

Delegate. This is difficult for some people, but I guarantee that when you are busy enough, you'll try it. Besides, similar to my experience with housecleaners, the personal investment in the smooth running of the household that each family member makes will help give them a sense of connectedness to their family.

When Jim and I were in about our fifth year of marriage, we were both working forty-plus hours per week and then traveling and performing concerts most weekends. Even though we shared the household responsibilities, it seemed that even the most minimal requirements began to choke me. In one of those "how do we reduce our stress" conversations, we decided to make a list of our respective responsibilities and switch for two weeks. I definitely got the better end of the deal.

We discovered that while Jim had to think of things like taking out the trash and mowing the grass once a week, paying the bills once a month, changing the oil and other maintenance on the car every few months, and then doing the taxes once a year, I was withering away with daily stresses like, "Do we have milk for breakfast?" "What should I thaw for dinner tonight?" "Do we have clean underwear?" "Is there any toilet paper?" "Did I pick up his suit from the dry cleaners?" These weren't earth-shattering stresses, but they were unrelenting everyday stresses. After our two-week switch, my very gracious mate and I came up with a redistribution of responsibilities that evened out the amount of daily, weekly, monthly, and yearly stress points.

This form of delegating was a really successful tool for us. If you have children, they can easily be integrated into the system with a balanced selection of responsibilities as well. Considering each individual's strengths and abilities will help match the right chore with the right personality. Jim is best with short-range jobs because his attention span is shorter. I'm better with detail and organizing, and he's better with the physical jobs like vacuuming and trash collecting. We established the rule that when one cooks, the other cleans up. Delegating will also help eliminate a lot of undesired nagging because everyone knows his or her job and is responsible to do it.

There is just one tiny potential problem here. Once everyone has been taught or knows how to execute his respective jobs, you have to let them do them, and do them their way. I discovered early in our marriage that when I asked Jim to help by making up the bed, he would do it, but I wouldn't like the way he did it. So I would come along behind him and do it over. This sent him the message that he might as well not try if I was just going to re-do it anyway. I should have let him make the bed his way and used the time it gave me for something more valuable than criticizing or repeating the job. While I'm not suggesting license for lazy work, I am suggesting that it is important to keep a perspective and not allow a perfectionist nature to demotivate the delegatees.

Chores may seem endless at times, but it helps to take them a step at a time. My mom always told me that the dishes get washed one dish at a time.

Instead of seeing a sinkful, it is better to see them as a series of one dish after another. Chores and responsibilities are the same. They will eventually get done, one thing at a time.

These three management tips will help simplify the process, but keep in mind they are suggestions, and that coloring outside the lines once in a while is healthy too. Don't be afraid to disregard brazenly the progressive domestic tools and insult flagrantly time-saving inventions like the dishwasher by enjoying a few moments of conversation beside your mate or child, as you both, hands wet with cleansing water, enjoy the rite of dish washing together, one dish at a time.

COOKING

Cooking is not just an everyday task, but three times a day. Three times the opportunity to persevere creatively, and this doesn't include the numerous snacks consumed in a twenty-four-hour period.

Growing up, my cousin and I began to pray for our future husbands as we discovered that the only dish we could execute successfully in the kitchen was cinnamon toast. While I received many great cookbooks as wedding gifts, I quickly came to the end of my vocabulary as a cook in the early months of my marriage.

I felt a certain seventh-grade-home-ec burden to cook full meals of meat, vegetable, starch, green, and dessert each evening, rotating the selection of meats between chicken, pork, seafood, and various beef options. Because I had no dishwasher, I quickly discovered the joys of crock-potting. However, just about anything tossed in and cooked for five or six hours tasted like mystery-mush, so while it simplified, it also nauseated.

When my older sister got married, she attempted to cook with leftovers in mind. A few months into her marriage she hadn't successfully netted any leftovers, but had a loving husband who was several pounds heavier. As they honed their communication skills, she discovered that he was afraid she would be hurt if he didn't eat all that she had prepared, so he just kept eating. He has lost the weight now, and she enjoys the benefits of leftovers.

Because I was a child of the canned vegetable era, I'll never forget my surprise at coming upon fresh vegetables in the grocery store for the first time. As a new wife, I was mystified as to how those bright-green hard beans made the transformation into mushy brown ones, not to mention dealing with the head of broccoli that wouldn't fit in any of my shiny new bridal pans. I am flushed with embarrassment.

My pride was restored when a friend told me of her roommate in college. She had led a princess-like life, and college was a hard reality for this beauty with no life skills. Their first time in the kitchen together, my friend stood in awe as she watched her friend, following the instructions on the slice-and-bake cookies wrapper, begin to "grease bottom of pan." Not wanting to interrupt this work in progress, she watched as the pretty girl then proceeded to "place cookies on oven rack." If it hadn't been for my friend, the fledgling cook would have starved that year.

I might as well go ahead and confess that in the twenty years following my wedding day I have discovered that I am just basically in no way motivated in the culinary craft. Therefore, my need to persevere in this dreaded everyday task is even more pronounced.

One thing that has helped me is finally to land on some favorite recipes. This takes time at first, but after scouring cookbooks and dialing long distance to family members and begging for help, I eventually developed a collection of reliable recipes that I could put into a rotating menu. They were recipes I didn't have to think about because they were tested and proved reliable, or survivable in my case.

Aside from the brilliant idea I had of equipping my husband with the ability to prepare a selection of meals, I have also partnered with friends on occasion. Each of us cooks a double recipe, and then we swap half for half. Variety and a feeling of community in one Tupperware.

Another strategy I have employed is that of power cooking. I would take Monday mornings and prepare three or four things that could be eaten during the week. A selection of casseroles that could easily be supplemented by fresh fruit or salads got us through one summer. Favorite soups made up in large quantities with freshly baked cornbread every few days carried us through the fall. Thai, Indian, Mexican, Italian, and health food themes provided variety and helped keep things interesting in the winter.

My favorite discovery caused me to add to my meager collection of household appliances. Recently, we committed to a daylight fast for Lent. During this time, we discovered the joys of juicing. This wonderful little contraption reduces the complex challenge of ingesting the recommended daily amounts of fruit and vegetables into a simple ten-minute exercise.

With the purchase of a modestly priced juicer and one book containing general information on juicing and a plethora of recipes, I was equipped to simplify my life in a big way. While I may not be very interested in cooking, I am close to obsessed with eating well, and this new habit has distinctly reduced my worrying and fretting time.

Making out menus, cooking ahead, freezing foods, juicing, sharing the cooking load, and occasionally eating out can all be helpful in persevering in the kitchen. Once again, keeping in mind the "who" on the other side of the need will help keep this task perseverable. When all else fails, cinnamon toast with a smile is a reliable fail-safe, and I always keep a can of black-eyed peas at the ready in the pantry.

GIFT GIVING

The everyday task of gift giving can be persevered rather than feared. Usually, around three weeks before my birthday, my husband begins the subtle "What do you want for your birthday?" questioning. While he has had many successful gift-giving events, they all followed the first Valentine's Day that we were married when he gave his mother and his brand-new bride the same red carnation with red pipe cleaner heart in a white vase purchased at the grocery store on the way home.

It is a little unfair to him, because I am hard to buy for. Even when I was a child, there were problems. One Christmas, I asked for a "Saucelito" doll. My cousin had a "Thumbelina" doll, but I couldn't remember that so it came out "Saucelito." My parents diligently quizzed me on what sort of doll she was, and I replied with a curt "Santa Claus will know." On Christmas morning my four-year-old heart broke and fell in love at the same moment. My parents' efforts paid off. It wasn't a Thumbelina, but she was beautiful and I loved her instantly.

In another year of potentially disappointing Christmas presents, I had asked for one of those small cars that had peddles in it (like a bicycle, but not). We were at my cousins' house for Christmas, and that morning, I ran right to the car. It was actually intended for my two-years-older male cousin, and since he hadn't asked for it, he and I were convinced that it was mine. Our parents struggled with a convincing story, and my mom distracted me with the medical kit I had also asked for.

So last birthday, when my husband hadn't brought up the gift subject, I got curious. One day I asked him point blank if he had my birthday under control and he gave me a confident smile and said, "All taken care of." I worried. I hadn't dropped any hints at all, and my girlfriends confessed that he hadn't conferred or confided in them. About two nights before my birthday, he began to shake with repressed laughter in bed. With no questioning at all, he blurted out, "Bagel-wide toaster. I was going to buy you a bagel-wide-toaster for your birthday." His laughter revealed that he had come to his senses and realized that a bagel-wide toaster plugs in and that you never give your wife something that plugs in for her birthday. Due to the fact that said occasion was now in less than thirty-six hours, I granted him an extension and several weeks later, a beloved prayer bench that I had seen in an antique store in Pennsylvania was delivered to my front door. As he received the tears of a grateful wife, he also presented me with a lovely bagel-wide toaster.

After discussions with many other panicked husbands and disappointed wives, the idea for the Gift Card File came to me. You start with a three-by-five box and put dividers labeled with the name of each member of the family in it. When son sees the perfect baseball glove at the store, he is encouraged to go home and write it on a card and then put it in his file. When daughter sees the most divine pair of shoes, she is told to record size, color, and store on her card in the file. Mom might see a great gift in a store, or she might request a night out for dinner and a movie or having her bed made for her for a week or control of the channel changer for a weekend or many other creative options. The whole idea is to build a resource for any gift-giving occasion that has a variety of ideas and costs from which other family members can "shop." It encourages thinking of the person behind the need, as well as simplifying the task.

Christmas presents seem to present their own horn-of-plenty stresses. In our fervor to accomplish the what, when, and where of our Christmas shopping, we can easily lose sight of the who of the season. Simplifying our approach can help give us time to see more clearly.

Recently, our extended family decided that for Christmas gifts, instead of everyone shopping for lots of small and possibly undesired gifts, we would select a price—for example, $200—and everyone would chip in and buy one big gift for each couple. Because so much effort goes into buying so many unwanted gifts, we were all glad to give this a try. My sister and brother-in-law got another chair for their dining room set, my parents got a power washer, my niece and her husband got a piece of furniture, and Jim and I got a stereo for the car. We rejoiced at not having to bring home those unwanted soap dishes, earrings, sweaters, or ties. We still bought small personal items like bath oil, or socks, or whatever for each others' stocking stuffers, but the major task of Christmas shopping was greatly simplified.

Theme Christmases can make shopping easier, too. The first year we owned our house we asked for lawn and garden items. We netted a hose, nozzle, weed whacker, leaf blower, and a variety of hand tools and work gloves. Another year we did a white theme and asked for white sheets, towels, socks, and candles. Anything to narrow the shopping field helps.

Another time-saving and sometimes money-saving idea is to catalog shop. Finding easily accessible catalogs and then exchanging wish lists can really make short work of a long chore. With a phone call you can order the gift and have it wrapped and shipped to the intended person, and still be sitting by the fireplace listening to Bing.

With our friends, we instituted the Christmas ornament tradition. Every year we give each other an ornament, and then each Christmas we are reminded of all of our friends when we decorate the tree (or trees).

Paying attention and knowing the receiver of the gift is most desirable in all gift giving. (Think prayer bench, not bagel-wide-toaster.) When there is time or an important person involved, gifts that say "I paid attention" are always more appreciated than overpriced gifts of insignificant meaning. One of my favorite simple gifts to give is five smooth stones. The Old Testament story says that when David went out to challenge Goliath, he stopped by the brook and picked up five smooth stones. Equipped with these, he went out and killed the giant. I like to find a special container for the stones—like an old antique silver bowl—and then enclose a note encouraging the person to give the rocks names that will help him to defeat the giants in his own life. Peace, contentment, joy, simplicity.

Because it just isn't always possible to personalize gifts distinctly, I have found it handy to purchase unique things when I find them to have on hand for birthdays or other events that sneak up on me. I also try to keep some generic cards that I can write a birthday or any occasion message on. And each January, while the Christmas busyness is fading, I sit down and transfer birthdays, anniversaries, and special occasions to my new calendar. It sounds like I'm adding to your list of things to do rather than helping you simplify, but in all truth, these things will make the every-once-in-a-while task of gift giving simpler.

SIMPLE SUMMARY

If efficiency were the only goal of persevering in our everyday world, we could examine and learn from the incredibly focused life of the colonizing ant. In community, the ant develops what starts out as basically an underground cave into a finely tuned habitat. Food is brought in, the brood is cared for, and the queen is protected—all in a microclimate perfect for the ants. There are workers assigned to open or close a complex system of ventilation shafts as need be to control the climate. Eggs, larvae, and pupae are carried through the corridors into areas that suit their specific climatic needs. Those assigned as soldiers control the entrance to the habitat so that only things beneficial to the colony come in. As the hunting ants bring in prey, they hand them over to workers and immediately head for the exit to repeat the process. Workers responsible for nest hygiene singly focus on their job.[2] The result is a highly efficient yet soulless community. The ants teach us about efficiency, and while they are only doing what they were created to do, we as soul-imbued creatures have the opportunity to take what for ants is purely mechanistic and turn it into something that is personally meaningful. In the ant model, the chore becomes the goal, rather than the character resulting from perseverance. It is not contentment that is achieved, but resignation.

Simplifying our lives by persevering in the everyday is not simply a matter of refining a well-run machine. Implementing ergonomic techniques and practical helps, and even ant efficiencies, will direct us down the path of simplifying, but what resulting space is created will only help us reflect the image of God if we surrender to the process and let perseverance lead us to character.

3

FOCUSING ON
THE GOAL

Our ability to focus on the goal of reflecting the image of Christ in our lives can be equipped or tripped by our use of time. Good skills in this area will simplify our lives, while poor time management can cripple the goal. In the passage from Luke where Martha missed a "Jesus moment" and failed to focus on the goal, it was because her time priorities were out of order. The tyranny of the urgent had its long arms around her heart. The philosopher Goethe put it this way: "Things which matter most must never be at the mercy of things which matter least."

My father has been a "three-by-five card man" for as long as I can remember. Way before organizers and time-management systems were popular, my dad had a shirt pocket full of things to do, along with some blank cards should a new item come up. At one point he even carried around several colored felt-tip pens and developed his own system of prioritizing and organizing. There were piles of retired cards in his drawers or briefcases, and every Christmas I put a new package of possibilities in his stocking. When I was a sophomore in college, I had a defining moment with my dad on the subject of God's guidance that ended with a reference to those three-by-five cards. My then-boyfriend—now husband—had asked my dad for my hand in marriage three times and been met with a "no" all three times. The "no" had less to do with my choice of husband and more to do with my extreme youth. We started asking when I was eighteen years old and Jim twenty-two. We desperately held to the truth that honoring my parents meant waiting for their blessing on our marriage. But I'll admit that I was beginning to look up alternative definitions to "honor." In my exasperation that day, I said, "Dad, what do you want, a three-by-five card from God?" And Dad unflinchingly said, "Yes."

Little did I know that the three-by-five system of time management was actually one of the approved methods God used. He delivered what we all considered to be a circumstance that was a clear three-by-five card with our wedding date written on it, and we were married eight months later with my parents' blessing. They are so crazy about Jim now that once in a while I have to remind them that I am the daughter.

Hundreds of systems are available to help organize your approach to time. The most important aspect is to find the one that works for you. I watched my dad experiment with several organizer systems, and after thorough examination, they have all been tried and found wanting. He's back to the three-by-fives. They work for him, and as for me, they are a charming eccentricity that says "Dad," and a reminder of God's caring guidance in our lives.

I like visual images. Something I can see in my mind finds a quicker place in my heart. So as we attempt to focus on the goal by developing good time-management skills, I would like to use the analogy of a garden.

I have experimented with gardening over the past eight years and learned a lot about the joys and the disappointments. I frightened a young white Labrador in our neighborhood within an inch of his mortality when I looked out to see him digging up the first tiny rewards of my marigolds planted from seed. I learned about unplanned interruptions. When my first tomato plant gave forth its first fruit, I waited one day to harvest it and a bird pecked holes in it. I learned about procrastination. When I planted a lot of annuals—plants that last just one year—I learned the cost of instant but fleeting gratification.

Gardening has become a sophisticated science in the past few years, spawning catalogs and specialists telling you everything from what and how to plant to what to wear and shovel your dirt with. The accoutrements are charming, and the extensive advice is helpful, but gardening really is still about digging a hole in the dirt, putting in a plant, smashing as much of the dirt as possible back around the plant, washing your hands, and sitting back in the hammock to enjoy your efforts. But you can get so wrapped up in the process that you never enjoy the garden. The same is true of time management. We don't want the method to be so cumbersome that the goal is defeated. So whether you find a complex organizer or a calendar on the refrigerator or a pocket of three-by-five cards to be your favorite method, don't forget that it's not a complicated science. The contemplative hobby that allows for the freedom to get dirty, the discipline of maintenance, and the rewards of effort suggests four manageable areas of focus for gardening that also apply to time management. They are simply: (1) read, (2) seed, (3) weed, and (4) feed.

READ

There isn't a better way to conquer the claustrophobic blues of a cold winter night than sitting with a magazine filled with pictures of beautifully blooming gardens. Around February, when I've had enough of wool clothes and the snow watch report on television and I feel that I will burst if the sun doesn't make an appearance in my sky soon, I pull out all of my magazines and books on gardening, as well as my file filled with torn-out pages, old seed packets, and scribbled notes to myself listing successes and failures from my little plot in the backyard. These cold winter nights are the beginning of any winning garden: reading, or research and development. Because I and most people don't have the green gift that Nanny, my mom's mom, had of tossing a plant nonchalantly into a pile of dirt and harvesting flowers weeks later, we need to plan.

A garden that hasn't been considered until the day of planting will suffer the consequences of poor placement and selection, possibly poor soil, and will never reach its full productive capability. A small amount of planning and research will help prevent you from planting the delicate primrose, which can tolerate only shade and moist soil, next to the oriental poppy, which needs six hours or more of direct sun and prefers well-drained soil. In my yard, a little attentiveness to my two miniature schnauzers' habit of chasing each other under the screened-in porch would have saved many daylilies from being wretchedly shred last spring.

As it relates to time management, this first area of reading covers everything from planning to setting goals and priorities. This is possibly the most important part of managing your time. In this area you establish an overall look at your life goals and how to move toward them. In garden terms, you assess your soil and determine what you want to grow. It isn't as much about doing and accomplishing as it is planning and researching. Establishing a mission statement, which we will discuss in depth in the Soul section, would be done here. Also, determining long-range goals of career plans, family vacations, purchase of a car or house, and the amount of time needed to apply toward reaching each goal should be considered. In this step, you can even decide on family policy on things like nights out and nights at home, amount of church and community participation, one-on-one time with your mate, and visiting with extended family. As much as you want to get your hands in the dirt and start accomplishing, this time of planning is the foundation to all uses of your time.

Such important plans must be grounded in values and life priorities and marinated in prayer. One of my favorite life verses is Jeremiah 29:11 where the Lord says, "I know the plans I have for you, . . . plans to prosper you and not to harm you, plans to give you hope and a future" (NIV). Couple this with David's words of advice in Psalm 37:4–5: "Delight yourself in the LORD and he will give you the desires of your heart. Commit your way to the LORD; trust in him and he will do this" (NIV), and you have the context in which to develop plans and goals.

I have changed and reassessed these plans and goals in my own life many times. I've often felt like Moses in the wilderness, wandering around a desert without a map. But then in a quiet investment of time spent with a full teapot in the morning, my heart felt impressed in one direction or another. Just as was the case for Moses, there will be limited supply and vision. Enough sustenance each day and the promise of a place of belonging will carry hopes into goals.

Once you have considered these crucial life issues, you will know enough about your life garden to proceed to step number two, *seed.*

SEED

The actual connection of hand to dirt for a gardener is like the sound of a starter's pistol for a runner. After the dark inside-ness of winter, the opportunity to be outside and rummage through earth's blanket with gloved or ungloved hands is pure elixir. In anticipation of this joy, my friend Debbie and I will fill a van with plants from a nursery and coo over them as if they were treasures from Tiffany's. We push the season every year and end up loosing a few delicate florae in our haste, but we can't wait to place something into waiting soil. We have been known to be so excited as not to allow the sunlight's fade to moonlight to impede our progress, and have planted by the glow of headlights from our cars.

While there are many other aspects to gardening, at least three appropriate to our discussion, this is the part that most people consider actual gardening. It is the same with time management. This is the part where you will feel movement. This is the practical application of the plan developed in the reading phase; it is filling in the garden.

As we begin to fill in the calendar, we need to take a few things into consideration. First, the facts are that there are 24 hours in a day and 168 hours in a week. You might want to make a list of items like sleeping, grooming, working, preparing and eating food, and any other daily activities. List how many hours you spend each day on each specific task, and then multiply each by 7 and subtract from 168. This is how many hours you have left for things like hobbies, social activities, church, volunteering, mate or child time, watching television, relaxing, and so forth, in a week. The results can be a rude awakening. I often feel like there has been a loaves-and-fishes miracle done on my hours as it seems like I have way more than 168 hours worth of activity in a seven-day span. Keep in mind that this exercise is not meant to set you up for a rigid schedule, but it is a perspective builder as you actually begin to manage your time.

Secondly, make lists. I have even gone so far as to make lists of my lists. That may sound like it's defeating the purpose of simplifying our lives, but it gave me a starting place to organize and identify where I was spending my time. The process of writing down the things that must be done helps you to focus, and there is a certain reward in being visibly able to cross things off as they are finished. One of the biggest stresses in time management is the fear that you will forget to do something that is important. With lists, you are downloading all of the little lost post-it notes scattered around your brain. Once you have all of those seemingly unrelated and overwhelming tasks written down, you can begin to tame the wild, out-of-control, time-eating beast.

After you have made out a to-do list, you must prioritize before you can attack. Keep in mind the Goethe quote from the beginning of this chapter and identify the truly important things on the list. And because you spent time in the reading, or research and development phase, you will have overall goals that will filter your thinking. Be flexible. Sometimes it will be more important to sacrifice what seems urgent for what is truly important.

In a garden, planting annuals, which bloom right away but must be planted each year, will give you instant gratification, but the long-term investment in perennials, which may not bloom the first year and cost more than annuals but last for several years, will reduce your time spent planting and your overall yearly expense. It is wiser to plant mostly perennials and fill in with annuals. Similarly, in prioritizing your things to do, you'll want the majority of your time to be spent on "perennials" or long-term investments, and then fill in with the "annuals," or short-term investments. You could easily fill a list with short-term things because they must be done, and sacrifice time on the things that have a longer-range return and either floating or no deadlines.

Perennial time investments would be things like what Stephen Covey terms "not urgent, but important."[1] The activities that contribute to your long-range goals established in the read phase should have priority. They might be things like making a budget, shopping for a full week's menu, paying taxes quarterly if you are self-employed, vacation, time getting to know a neighbor, or personal spiritual time. These activities might contribute to a goal of being wise financially or goals for more quality time with friends and family as well as God. Long-term investments will save time in the long run and align with life priorities.

The short-term time investments, or annuals to fill in with, would be those daily and weekly things that must be done to keep life going. They have to be on the list, but efficient planning will keep them from devouring your time. And if you have things like "breathe" and "eat" on your list and they never get crossed off, you are too busy and your priorities are probably out of order.

Now that you have a list and it is prioritized, you are ready to accomplish things. The next step might seem minor, but it can have a great impact on your productivity. Identify the time of day you work best. I know that when I wake up in the mornings, I am only good at task-oriented things. My brain doesn't function fully until lunch. So, I take the morning to do things like laundry, dishes, phone calls, exercise, and errands. In the afternoon and early evening, I tackle writing and contemplative tasks. I've also found that when I'm pushing deadlines, I work well between nine at night and three in the morning. Those feel like "free" hours for me because I'm not ignoring my husband or any phone calls, the house is quiet, and I can be creative and write or paint. Obviously, I can't maintain that schedule indefinitely, but I do find it invigorating occasionally.

Knowing these things about myself frees me to schedule my time accordingly. I don't feel guilty about inserting an early lunch with friends because I know that my productive time will be after that anyway. I don't worry about emptying the dishwasher at night because I know I will need that type of project to start off my morning. The idea of getting to know yourself and your "clock" will help you develop rhythms and routines, not lunatic legalisms.

If this much organizing has gone against your natural personality type, hang on. It will become second nature eventually, and the initial investment of concentration will be worth it.

WEED

The first year I gardened, I didn't know how to tell the weeds from the seeds. The problem is, when they start out, they look a lot alike. Pleasantly green little stems with bilateral leaves tentatively stared up at me, and I heard "Let me live." It wasn't until wily vines threateningly wrapped themselves around my precious peonies that I sensed a problem. They were fairly easy to pull away, but the weeds that covertly mingled in with my blue salvia threatened to take the blooms with them if I pulled them out. So to rid my garden of this problem the following year, I educated myself on what weeds looked like, identified them, and tried to eliminate them early on. The mere fact that I even knew to be on the watch for them was probably my best defense.

In time management, weeds threaten our perfectly planned lives all the time. As with the garden, knowing to watch for them is a good beginning. So many times I get to the end of my day and say, "Where did the time go?" In most of these cases, weeds have made a move on my blooms.

Let's identify some potential weeds.

Distractions whittle away the moments. They come in a variety of forms and stealthily sneak up on you. You are on your way out the door, and the phone rings. You pick it up and the next thing you know, you have spent twenty minutes chatting. As you are walking to the car, you see the mail and stop to read it. The Publishers' Sweepstakes has sent you notice that you must return your entry today, so you stop and fill it out.

Trivial time-wasters devour hours. You sit down to watch a show on television, and one show turns into an entire evening. You go to the mall for a pair of black shoes and look at every other color, too. You pull out a magazine to look at a recipe and end up reading articles on how to eliminate ear fat. You go online to search one thing and spend time searching lots of other interesting subjects as well.

Procrastination can leave a to-do list with no check marks. With as many things as we are going to do "tomorrow," we'll need more than twenty-four hours. Putting "it" off adds compounding interest to an already high stress account. It is like falling victim to point-of-purchase buying—we come across something that we "must do" right now, which pulls us away from what we were doing, making us procrastinate completing that task. But as in impulse shopping, if we were to stop and evaluate, we would see that what distracted us might only be disguised as important. In Charles Hummel's hugely popular booklet *Tyranny of the Urgent*[2] he says that we leave a trail of unfinished tasks in our lives and our quiet moments are haunted by them. In reminding us of Jesus' example, he quotes from John 17:4 where Christ said, "I have finished the work which thou gavest me to do" (KJV). Living in the confidence of what the Father called him to do, Christ did the work set before him as it came with no procrastinating.

Just say "no." One of the first words children learn to say and say with conviction is *no.* Somewhere in our developing into young women, we confused godliness with niceness, and niceness meant never saying *no.* We are faced with "yes" and "no" opportunities several times a day. If left untamed, this weed will choke the life out of any other plants in the garden. An appropriate and pleasant "no" that thanks for the opportunity but graciously declines is a sign of a woman who has focused on the goal by wisely considering her time and its use.

Every garden has some weeds. But the sooner we identify them, the easier they are to pull. The longer we wait, the deeper the roots and the more tenacious the weed. In the worst case, a weed can grow so insidiously that when it is pulled it out, we will have to sacrifice the bloom with the tare. On the other hand, conscientious care for our garden, or schedule, will leave it free to bloom its best.

FEED

I am a good starter when it comes to gardening. I love to plan and plant, (read and seed), and I find weeding relaxing. The only problem with this zeal is that I got carried away one year and put in so many plants that I depleted the soil and reduced the yield potential on my flowers. Jim, being a better finisher than starter in the garden, saved our summer by carefully measuring out and applying weekly fertilizer and water to the hungry plants.

In our time management we can be guilty of the same thing. We commit to so many wonderful sounding projects that we have limited resources to give to any of them. That is why this last step, *feed,* is so essential.

A garden that has been fed by fertilizer or compost benefits from having nutrients outside of itself to draw upon. An undernourished plant produces only the basics: spindly stem and leaf and a green exterior. It is not so much that the plant will die without this feeding, but it just won't reach its fullest potential.

We, as God's most precious creation, are so much the same. As we consider simplifying our lives by using time more efficiently, we must not over-program ourselves so that there is no time for personal and spiritual feeding. When we forget to plan for this, we will run out of ourselves and have nothing to draw on. We will accomplish the necessities but never bloom at our fullest potential.

While we will discuss some of this topic in greater detail later in Part II, "Soul," there are three specifics I would like to deal with as it relates to feeding ourselves in our time management: (1) relationships, (2) new ideas and opportunities, and (3) personal growth and maintenance. They may seem like expendables in an already busy life, but don't be deceived. This is irreplaceable fuel. In the reading phase, we planned for it. In the feeding phase, we live it.

Relationships. It is easy for me to become involved in something and to guard my time so preciously that I miss out on the energy and joy of relationships. But the grounding and perspective gained in connected living far outweigh the cost in time. It doesn't always mean giving up an entire day to be with someone, although this can be healthy, too. I have found that keeping a supply of postcards beside my desk facilitates contact in one way. When I think about someone, or have those middle-of the-night periods of open eyes, writing a short note to someone carries my spirit. I also maintain several phone friendships that feed me. A short conversation keeps me informed on my friend's life, and my friend on mine. I have found E-mail to be particularly handy for staying in touch with some people, and the privacy of it has caused us to discuss deeper things than we might have felt comfortable with in each others presence. While none of these three ideas will place you physically in relationship, they will still feed your need for community.

More advance planning is necessary to facilitate time in the presence of others. Weekly, I try to plan for two lunches out with some pals. Because Jim and I work at home, we need to get out to see other humans, so we go out for dinner with friends a lot. On Wednesday nights we try to go out with a different couple after Bible study, which is a convenient way to spend time with people we don't see often.

Since our families live in other states, we really have to plan long-range to make time to see them. Sometimes we'll meet at one family's home, or we'll go to neutral ground and rent a condo or two at the beach. The longer

I am alive, the more I cherish the times with family. When I was growing up, my mother, her mother, all of her sisters, and all of the children tried to spend time together each summer. The time I spent at the feet of these southern matriarchs while they were frying cornbread, playing canasta, or telling stories and sipping Cokes on the porch is requisitely woven into my own maturation as a woman.

We all have daily, weekly, monthly, and yearly relationships to maintain. You will find that there will be those who are easily and automatically in your routine and those you have to make a conscious effort to include. Generosity in this area will never cause regret.

New ideas and opportunities. Spending time discovering ways to help advance your life goals is essential. Once the goals are decided upon in the reading step, they need to be pursued. Because life and routines can become stagnant, we need to keep the waters flowing. There are seasons in our lives when something works to further our goals, but what has worked before may need adapting at some point. When we were traveling and performing for extended periods of time, we realized that our old ways of traveling when we were gone for just weekends didn't sustain us when we were gone for weeks at a time. We took some time to develop new habits and policies to help feed ourselves in this new circumstance. We searched out wonderful historic hotels and treated ourselves to one every few nights. We decided we could no longer subsist on three fast-food meals a day and established the "one sit-down restaurant a day" policy. Just a few adjustments refreshed us enough to feed us while we traveled.

Taking time to reflect on how you are working toward your goals and infusing new ideas will help you avoid burnout and keep you from becoming a withered, underfed plant.

Personal growth and maintenance. We can become so busy giving and taking care of that we allow ourselves to suffer. When we are spent, we have nothing to give anybody else anyway. We must schedule personal and intimate time with the Lord and time to care for our bodies. It will not just happen on its own. This will include everything from spiritual disciplines to routine doctor appointments. It covers time spent in a bookstore looking for books that help facilitate quiet time as well as the quiet time itself. It includes exercise, haircuts, and hot baths. Building these things into our routines as foundational elements will keep them from being squeezed out by the busyness of our lives.

My parents had a beautiful rose garden when they lived in Kentucky. They spent a long time learning about roses and what type would thrive in their yard. They had hybrids, florabundas, tea roses, climbers, and American beauties. When they planted them, they dug down several feet and added sand for good drainage and bone meal for root enhancement. They also enriched the soil to provide nutrients to feed the plants. In the early evenings, my mother would lovingly pull weeds from around her roses and faithfully fertilize them. This rose garden rewarded them with rooms full of beautiful blooms in various stages of opening. Soft antique colors and screaming velvet reds found themselves in everything from bud vases to huge glass jars. They stood tall or floated delicately. A well-fed garden will reward you with a profusion of blooms, and in the same way, when you allow time for personal "feeding," you will be rewarded with personal growth and blooming.

SIMPLE SUMMARY

As we discuss focusing on the goal of reflecting the image of Christ as it relates to our body, or environment, we see that a life of frenetic, out-of-control busyness will net us frazzled, out-of-control lives. Not only that, if we haven't put any forethought into our priorities and life goals, we might be like Martha and miss a Jesus moment.

Similarly, using the garden analogy, we know that a beautiful and thriving garden does not happen by a fortunate collocation of plants and nutrients that have built-in force fields to protect against weeds. Unplanned, uncared-for gardens will eventually revert to their wild state and resemble anything but something intentional. We will have a healthy and productive garden only if we read, seed, weed, and feed. For our lives to be lived intentionally, we need to apply these same good gardening techniques to our time management.

There is a picture in my head of my dream garden. It is terraced and full of botanical delights that show off in all seasons. It is well maintained. It has the perfect amount of morning sun and afternoon shade. It produces maximum blooms, and I can smell them from my back door. It doesn't rely on the artifice of lawn ornaments or exotic high-maintenance plants. It is planted in good soil; and its roots go deep, and its blossoms abound.

There is a picture in the First Psalm of the person who delights in the law of the Lord. That person is like a tree planted by streams of water that yields fruit and doesn't wither. In all that person does, he or she prospers.

4

SUMMARY OF PART I

There is a stretch of maybe four blocks called the Village within walking distance of my house. It has been evolving in the seven years we have lived here. A famous Nashville pancake restaurant, a used bookstore, a cobbler, a wonderful import movie theater, a disco-looking throwback haircuttery, and a hardware store selling phonographs and Three Dog Night eight tracks are some of the highlights of the Village. There was also an unusual shop that I had gone into a couple of times in search of birthday gifts for lateral-thinking friends. I referred to it as "Bamboo K-Mart" because it carried mostly inexpensive trinkets of mostly Asian influence. Bamboo back scratchers with bright red tassels on the end, wicker baskets, bobbing-head dolls, tea cups with oriental Kanji decoratively surrounding the rims, chopsticks in bright lacquered colors that came to lethal points, and shiny metal balls claiming to relieve stress covered dusty glass shelves that hovered over 1970s-style shag carpeting. Boxes were stuffed under display counters and piled to the ceiling. In general, it was a store you would not mistake for an architectural wonder, and you would never know it was there unless you were in the market for stress-relieving shiny metal balls.

We were walking through the Village one day after having been out of town for a while when we passed by the Bamboo K-Mart and noticed signs for a "closing" sale. It seems that some entrepreneurial bakers had gotten together and planned to open a French-style bread-and-cheese shop in that spot. I mourned for the bamboo store for a fleeting moment, then rejoiced at our good fortune, anticipating the breads and mouth-watering cheeses that would soon arrive.

We watched the progress from across the street in the pancake eatery on many mornings through the coming months. We saw as the bland facade of siding was pulled off the exterior to reveal two gables with windows perched at the top. They were settled in a jumble of painted brick and old slogans. Within days the non-architectural exterior was transformed into a charming ochre-colored Provençal delight. We anticipated and attended the grand opening, when they invited people to come sample their snacks at no charge. I stood in the middle of the floor squinting my eyes and trying to remember the crowded shelves of knickknacks that had inhabited the space only months before. The corporate drop ceiling had been removed, exposing the beautiful skeletal structure of beams, pipes, and roof and allowing light to pour in through the two newly discovered gables. After looking up and enjoying the transformation, I remembered the shag carpeting and dropped my eyes. Not one shabby strand in sight. The larger eating area was floored by a herringbone-patterned brick, and the serving and entry area welcomed guests with a random pattern limestone. Both shined with a hand-waxed patina and I ran to tell one of the owners how much I appreciated their investment in an interesting interior. With the grin of a successful archaeologist, he smiled and said, "Isn't it amazing? All of this was here; we just unburied it." The beautiful structural ceiling was revealed when they removed the oppressive drop ceiling, the charming gables appeared when they shed the exterior skin like siding, and the one-of-a-kind floors were freed when the shag carpeting was shed. By removing everything that didn't look like a French bakery, this environment began to reflect the image of a patisserie in Provence.

As we say "yes" to the journey God invites us on, we discover that there are things we must shed in order to reveal the wonders of his image in us more clearly. In Part I, we have begun this shedding process by simplifying our environment.

The clutter and possessions of this life weigh us down and make for a burdened passage. We must reduce. The responsibilities of the everyday can be overwhelming and tedious. We must do more than endure; we must creatively persevere. When time and its demands control us, we must stop and focus by instead managing our time. As we take a proactive part in simplifying in body, we must post these things on our hearts.

WORKING IT OUT

1. Simplicity: peace, contentment, freedom from complexity or affectation, ease, lack of hindrance, clarity, definition, wholeness. Which words most describe the simplicity you long for in your life?

2. Do you fit your skin? Or do you at least recognize that you were designed intentionally? What are some things that might need carving away as you begin to simplify in order to better reflect the image of God in your life?

3. Take the "Clutter Quiz." Answer "yes" or "no" to the following humorous questions to help identify if you are a hoarder, a pack-rat, or a procrastinator in desperate need of "de-cluttering."

   • You save the rubber bands off of newspapers, the pins in packaged shirts, and plastic dry cleaning bags.
   • You save popsicle sticks for that project someday.
   • You still have the instruction manual for your hair dryer.
   • You have two or more nonfunctioning umbrellas.
   • Your basement is filled with cardboard boxes in case you have to mail something.
   • You have clothes in your closet that neither look good nor feel good but were a good deal.
   • You have tubes of lipstick in colors you hate but save in case you change your mind.
   • You have fondue forks but no fondue pot.
   • You have coupons that expired at least six months ago.
   • When you have new tires put on your car you save the old ones as backups.
   • You trip on your old manual typewriter when reaching for your nightgown.

- You save unlightable candles to someday melt down and make new ones.
- You have a service for twelve of Arby's Christmas mugs.
- You bought this book to read two years ago.
- You save single earrings in case you pierce your nose someday.
- You have fabric scraps from the Easter dress you made your five-year-old daughter, who is ten now.
- You have sheets in your linen closet for which you have no beds (i.e., you have twin sets but only queen size beds).
- You're saving anything because someday it might be worth something.
- You have shoe polish in colors that you have no shoes in.
- You have a snow shovel, even though you live in Miami.

Scoring: based on the total number of "yes" responses.

0–5   Go to the thrift store and buy some junk.

6–10   You may need to do some spring cleaning.

11–20   Stop reading and start tossing.

4. List five mundane tasks in your daily life and consider ways to make them more "perseverable." How can you make them fun? Can they be combined with other tasks? Can they be more effectively accomplished by delegating?

5. Managing your time is like maintaining a garden. In the analogy of read, seed, weed, and feed, which area has been neglected in your time management? Is your garden under siege by weeds? Is it underplanned? Underfed?

6. I say no:

(never)   1   2   3   4   5   (easily)

(Possible reasons for "never": "I thought it would make me look selfish," when it can actually be the opposite, or "I honestly do want to rescue everyone," which leads to burnout.)

7. You are a one-thousand-dollars-per-day consultant. Write yourself a letter with suggestions on where to begin making changes in your time management.

Prayer: Oh God, help me simplify in body. May I throw off the stuff, the excess earthly somethings that overburden or distract me in this journey. May I find joy and sustenance in the everyday, seeing not as with earthbound eyes, but divinely inspired vision of the heart. May my "must-be's" be transformed by the renewing of my mind into important things that conform me more to Your image. May You, God, who makes everything holy and whole, continue to make me so.

BODY: AT A GLANCE

- We were created to reflect the image of God. Some things may need to be carved away so that his image is seen more clearly.
- The pattern: Hebrews 12:1.
- Reduce the clutter—lean, clean and wean. Detach from things.
- Persevere in the everyday—persevere, not endure. Incline yourself to contentment. Make it fun, consolidate, delegate.
- Focus on the goal—time management. Read, seed, weed, and feed.

PART II.

SOUL:

SIMPLICITY IN OUR RELATIONAL/ EMOTIONAL WORLD

"She who reconciles the ill-matched threads of her
life, and weaves them gratefully into a single
cloth—it's she who drives the loudmouths from the
hall and clears it for a different celebration where
the one guest is You."
—Rainer Maria Rilke

"Let us take care not to participate too much
in all that is said and done, and not to absorb too
much of it, because this is a great source of
distraction. . . . Thus we shall always keep the
depths of our souls free and balanced, and we
shall cut off thoroughly the futile things which
embarrass our hearts, and which prevent them
from turning easily to God."
—François Fenelon

OK, so maybe I should have brought along a pitcher to make the lemonade in. That way, I would have been prepared all the way around. But don't you just hate it when people try to patronize you in difficult situations with pithy little sayings like, "When life hands you lemons, make lemonade"? This is when I begin to snarl, and my husband has to make excuses for me like, "She's on medication with side effects" or "Isn't that the cutest family trait she has where she foams at the mouth when she's really happy?"

We started out on a trip to Illinois where our band had been invited to play at an outdoor music festival. We loaded the rented RV with the usual necessities, as well as some refrigerator treats. Just this once, I hadn't settled for the niceties of boxed cookies or spongy-cakey things. I had labored long and hard over a lovely concoction of "cranberry-strawberry fruit delight"—Jello. Thirty minutes into our trip, I went to peer into the small refrigerator; and when I opened the door, the "delight" made a flying leap for freedom. While bracing myself on the floor of an RV traveling at sixty miles an hour and rubbing a lovely sunrise-red stain into the gold shag carpeting, I should have begun to smell lemons.

When we finally arrived at the campsite where RV hookups and sanitary dumps had been promised, we were informed that there were no such resources. Because we were inexperienced "RV'ers" we didn't fully comprehend the severity of our situation. Two more days into the adventure and an overwhelming toxic odor signaled the NEED for a sanitary dump. We were told there was a site off the grounds that you couldn't miss. We promptly missed it. After driving past one cow pasture after another, my resourceful husband decided he should at least get out and take a look at the "exit valve." In a moment of uninformed action, he opened the chamber and proceeded to receive three days worth of unpleasantness all over his personhood. He did not smell like lemons.

Well, the RV did smell better, and so did Jim after we hosed him off. We quickly returned to the campsite where we were to perform shortly. I began to walk to the stage and, for the first time, the reality of being at an outdoor festival where it had rained for two weeks hit me square in the face. And in the legs. And in the mouth. And everywhere else free-flying mud could connect with me. Mud. That slimy, good-for-nothing gook sent to this time and place to irritate me. And I began to get grumpy. It seemed that there was nothing but slime in my life. With each sloshing step I began to sink lower into the abyss of "poor me," and the possibility of making lemonade became more and more remote. It seems that at the messiest points in our lives, the Holy Spirit does his most life-enhancing surgery on our souls. My pitiful self was transported from the depths of bad attitude into the presence of awe.

I looked at the mud and began to see it as the Native Americans had seen it many years before, when they saw provision. They built homes out of it that sheltered them from the sun in the summer and the wind and rains in the winter. Then I saw the mud as Christ had seen it when he walked the earth. He saw healing in the mud. He smeared it over a blind man's eyes and when they washed it off, he could see. I thought of Rodin, who saw art in the mud. He harvested the mud to sculpt with, and in a simple gesture he could capture the essence of the human form. This inevitably led me to think of the Master Designer—God, Very God—who saw life in the mud. He reached down and scooped up two big God-fists full of mud and began to fashion humankind out of it. He pressed his God-lips against our mouths, and all of time and history was changed when that breath stained our lips, and the God of all looked at the mud and said, "It is good."

It is only with our souls that we can identify mud as something more than slime. Our bodies identify it as an "oozing ick," but it is in our God-authored souls that we give it meaning. It can become more than mud. It becomes life.

Because we have souls, however, we have discovered that life can stink. And there is a lot of mud. Our feelings get hurt, we face disappointments, we get depressed, we don't want to leave the house, nothing seems worth the effort. Our dreams have been left somewhere between ingenue and soccer mom. We decide that even our perfume makes our hips look big. We are in the feeling world of the soul. And not just the soul, but the "she soul."

As women, we tend to take the mud life delivers personally. The tapestry that weaves our complex beings was designed with a heavy hand toward the interior. We receive life and take it down deep inside of us. What we reveal to the outside world is only a hazy image of our whole selves. Like ghosts after flashbulbs, the pale image only hints at the depths to be found on further investigation.

So how does mud become more? How do we regain our dreams and like our thighs? We must simplify our lives in our interiors, in our souls. To be sure, this gift of interiorness is surety and volatility. It is asset and liability. It is dead weight around our necks when it ravages the disparities of faithless life and an anchor when plumbing the verities and mysteries of faith-filled life. It is mud, *and* it is life.

Because it is both, it will take intentionality on our part to know it and be in control of it. David spoke to his soul in the Psalms and once told it to "bless the LORD" (Ps. 103:1, NASB), which in Hebrew meant to kneel, to adore God. Later he told it to "praise the LORD" (Ps. 146:1, NASB), and this time the Hebrew meant to rave clamorously. Our souls can be blatantly loud and reverently quiet. While our bodies are busy relating to our physical environment, our souls relate to our emotional environment, including how we relate to others and ourselves. As we simplify our lives and get to know our souls better, we learn how to take control of them rather than letting them control us. I can better be prepared for how to react to betrayal by a friend, or disappointment in my career, or my context in life, or my need for personal nurturing.

Unlike the body, which allows us actually to see things that we need to simplify, our souls are a step toward the deeper and unseeable side. We will measure our progress more by intuitive methods than touchable tasks. Our souls have clutter, but we can't just sell it at a yard sale. We must persevere in its everydayness, but by sacraments of simplicity instead of efficiency techniques. And finally, when we focus on the goal, we will search our hearts for interior motivators instead of our pockets for three-by-five cards.

I love the soul. Like a box turtle carries its shell, I carry my soul with me and enter at any time. It is that visceral part of our being that is difficult to surround with words, but it is the immaterial essence that animates our lives. *Elan vital.*

5

REDUCING THE
CLUTTER

When you are six, it is very hard to have more than one good friend at a time. Maybe you have a new one every day, but you only have one at a time. Your young heart hasn't been exposed to the explosive and implosive features of complex relationships. You are innocently content that the sharing of clover patches and popsicles can be the basis for lifetime friendships, and that is that.

Now that I am an officially fully grown woman, I am fortunate to be a giver and receiver in several relationships. The childhood friendships were precious, but the innocence and undiscovered territory of youth cannot compete with the comfort of a well-worn and familiar path found in the company of seasoned friendships.

God made and designed us with community in mind. Ecclesiastes 4:9–10 reminds us that "two are better than one, because they have a good return for their work: if one falls down, his friend can help him up. But pity the man who falls and has no one to help him up!" (NIV). Even more, we were created by a Creator who is relational. In the beginning, the three-in-one relationship that is the Trinity was present. The first few verses of Genesis 1 tell us that while God was speaking creation into being, the Spirit was hovering over the water. John's first chapter and verses tell us that the Word that became flesh, Jesus, was with God "in the beginning." The three in unique relationship were together when God said, "Let us make man in our image . . . male and female he created them" (Gen. 1:26–27, NIV). Relationships are at the center of who we are, because they are at the center of who God is.

RELATIONSHIPS

Relationships take up a large chunk of our soul life. While I firmly believe that we define ourselves by who we are as redeemed children of God, I also believe that is enfleshed by how we rub up against other people in relationship. This is a lot like the river rock and its relationship to the river. The rock is a hard, solid collection of mineral matter regardless of its relation to the river. But over time, it will become smooth and rounded *because* of its relationship to the river. God has placed us in relationships for that same reason. We are like river rocks at the bottom of a stream, and the relationships in our lives are the water that flows over us. Sometimes the water is calm and gentle, and you can see yourself clearly through these relationships. Other times, the stream is violent and turbulent, and not only do the waters get muddied, but we also get tossed about. It is a lifetime of these relationships that helps shape who we are and smooth off the rough edges of our character.

Because sometimes the stream can rub us the wrong way, the clutter in our souls is centered on the conflict we have in relationships. While there are other things that can add clutter to our emotional world, most things can eventually be traced back to problems in a relationship. We all have friends and family members who can be assets or emotional drains on our lives at different times. The emotional drains create clutter, and having good conflict management skills will help reduce that clutter and ultimately simplify our lives.

As adults, our relationships fall into one of seven categories: (1) family, (2) friends, (3) acquaintances, (4) soul mate, (5) mentor, (6) apprentice, and (7) former relationships. (We will discuss our most important relationship, which is with God, in detail in Part III, "Spirit.") Not only do all of our relationships fall within one of these categories, but a healthy soul world will have all seven represented in its life in some way. Each type of relationship adds something essential to our lives.

Family relationships give a sense of heritage, belonging, and legacy. This should be the place where we will find unquestionable love and acceptance.

Friendships give a sense of being peers that helps us to see ourselves in the context of life. They will be the company on the journey and provide everything from nurturing (Prov. 17:17) to "sharpening" (Prov. 27:17), counsel (Prov. 27:9) to faithful wounds (Prov. 27:6), and reliable intercession (Job 16:20–21).

Acquaintances provide a casual relief in the world of relationships. The surface involvement demanded by these low-maintenance encounters is the grout that fills in the holes in our lives.

For those of us who are married, our *soul mate* should be our husband. For those who are single, a soul mate will typically be a best girlfriend, and while this is different from a husband-wife relationship, it fulfills a similar role. These are life-sustaining relationships of arterial importance. They carry the most weight in all of the same areas as a friend, and the sense of completeness found here is unmatched in any other relationship.

The *mentor* role can be filled by an older and wiser woman of faith. When flesh and blood are unavailable, many times I have been mentored through books. I have found it comforting to discover that what I am going through has been endured before. While these can be formally arranged relationships, I have also found that many women have mentored me without knowing it. The wisdom and experience of women who have gone further down the road is essential.

The *apprentice* in your life needs the age and wisdom that you can offer. The experiences you've had may seem average or unimportant to you, but they are precious insights for those who come along behind you. As you have need for a mentor, someone needs you to mentor them. Your wisdom may be in the mere fact that you have lived longer and seen more. The apprentice in your life benefits from your 20/20 hindsight. This relationship will also help remind you of God's faithfulness in your own life over the years. As we are told he has comforted us, that we would comfort others (2 Cor. 1:1–4).

Former relationships are those people that for one reason or another are no longer in your life. They may have moved, died, or just faded out of your life because you don't have anything in common with them any more. In some cases, the relationship may have ended in unresolved conflict. In that case, do your best to go back and make right what can be made right. We will discuss this further when we talk about forgiveness, but it is important to recognize that relationships, no matter what kind, will leave their mark on your soul. As you place—and leave—the negative ones at God's feet and carry on the positive ones, they will make indelible contributions to who you become, and they will continue to be voices in your heart and mind that urge you onward.

I have only briefly described the healthy definitions of the seven types of relationships we encounter. The clutter begins to collect when any or many of these relationships are in conflict. The key to reducing this clutter is found in making wise relational investments and in honing our conflict-management skills.

MANAGING CONFLICT

Two steps must be taken to manage conflict. First, recognize that it is inevitable. Second, have a plan to handle it.

Conflict is inevitable. When I was barely old enough to ride a tricycle, I overreacted slightly and ran away from home, peddling with intent to the corner. My mother had broken the news to me that we were out of chicken noodle soup, and I defiantly put my hands on my hips and declared that I was leaving home. Fortunately, before I got to the corner, my sister came running after me with a misplaced can of the soup in question. I was spared the embarrassment of having my dramatic journey cut short, as I was not allowed to cross the street. This little overreaction was an early warning signal that I might be a little feisty, and it was definitely a hint that there would be conflict in my future.

Even good relationships will face conflict. James 1:2 tells us to consider it all joy when—not if—we encounter various trials. With all of the wonderful types of relationships we have discussed, it is inevitable that relational conflict is a sure "various trial." Relationships themselves are, by design, emotional entanglements. That is the joy and the flaw. Sometimes we become so entangled, and because we have hesitated to recognize or deal with the conflicts, we can't find the end of the string to pull in beginning to untangle the problem. So, as my friend says, we resort to cutting what we should have untied. Then the relationship is lost and will require much more work to reconcile. That is why we can't afford to pretend that everything is OK in an attempt to avoid dealing with conflict. We have to acknowledge it exists and then have a proactive plan to deal with it.

Have a plan. There aren't many things that keep me off balance as much as unresolved conflict. It affects my sleep because I wake up in the middle of the night and have conversations over and over in my head, justifying myself or my actions. And if I want to sleep, I have to take at least three or four emotional steps back and try to work toward resolve.

I've identified five things to help ease us toward resolution in our relational conflicts.

Seek first to understand, then to be understood. This is not always my first instinct. I want to tell my side so that they can *really* understand what happened. The simple anatomy of it is that we have two ears and one mouth and should use them accordingly. Proverbs 2:2 plainly instructs us to "make your ear attentive to wisdom, incline your heart to understanding" (NASB). If we start out trying to resolve a conflict defensively, we will inflame the conflict. The gracious gesture of listening first gives opportunity for true communication, and the quiet you create by not trying to talk over the other person is a calming quiet. So many times I have wasted words and anger by speaking before I have understood a situation. At least 50 percent of communication is listening. I remember being so frustrated by someone who hadn't returned a phone call relating to a time-defined matter. When they finally called, they were greeted by the acid of my tongue. I was quickly reduced when I found out they were delayed because of a death in the family. Wisdom is to incline your heart to understanding, then to be understood. Be quick to hear, slow to speak (James 1:19).

Name the problem. It is so easy to become sidetracked and lose sight of the root issue by digressing into side issues. One Saturday morning, when Jim and I were in mid-argument, there was a knock on our door. Jim huffed out of the room to answer it while I steamed in my chair. I overheard him deliver a humorous and brusque refusal of the evangelistic fervor of two zealous Jehovah's Witnesses. After he allowed them to give a short sentence or two, he said, "Look, as far as God goes, we're all set here," and he shut the door.

When he returned for round two of our schism, I was desperately trying to swallow my laughter. After both of us had a good cackle, we tried to get back to our discussion and neither of us could remember the original source of the problem. We had digressed so far from the point that we had begun to resort to the unfruitful generalizations of "you never" or "you always."

A lot of time and breath are wasted on unimportant subissues and the main problem goes unexposed and more lethal. It is like having a tooth with a cavity in it. You can polish the tooth, floss, rinse with a pain-numbing agent; but until the cavity is drilled and filled, the tooth is on its way to dying. The longer we allow the root of a problem to remain undealt with, the relationship is on it's way to dying. Walking in lifetime fellowship with someone will demand saying the hard things from time to time in order to eliminate the things causing the relationship to decay. Those who won't risk the temporary pain of honestly and vulnerably identifying the problem speak with their actions that the friendship is not that valuable to them.

Examine your heart. Pray and ask the Lord to help you discern right from wrong in this specific situation, and ask him to give you courage to own your part. I continue to be surprised at my aptitude for wretchedness. I've only begun to plumb the depths of my own wormlike potential. My mouth speaks so much quicker than my brain edits, and my self-serving and self-preserving actions reveal a heart that needs moment-by-moment grace. These things cause me to be the "friend in the wrong" on more occasions than I want. It's not always the big and dramatically obvious things, as much as the insidious ways we have of eroding someone else's confidence, or diluting their enthusiasm, or monopolizing the spotlight, or our general passive involvement in their life that eats at the foundation of a relationship.

Sometimes when we take a minute to check out our side of the conflict, we discover that the source of the problem was our own vulnerability. Being tired, sick, or in a state of low self-esteem will make us particularly prime for conflict. We tend to be overly sensitive and overreact. I know I'm entering the emotional "hurricane warning" stage, meaning *conditions are right* for a hurricane, when my responses to small conflicts are grossly out of proportion. The warning siren blows in our house, and Jim knows to batten down all hatches and secure any exposed glass. I'm not proud of this condition, but learning to identify it has begun to help me prepare and react better, and even laugh a little. A little. And of course, I watch the calendar to prepare for hormonal havoc. There isn't much that is more aggravating than when a husband says, "Honey, is it that time?" in the middle of a disagreement. I much prefer to begin my rants with "I know I'm hormonal right now, but that isn't the reason I'm mad at you for breathing in the same room as me."

I can see these things in the quiet of a nonconfrontational moment, but in haste or heat I resort to familiar patterns that ravage relationships. When the Spirit's nudging—and sometimes *strong* nudging—breaks open my heart to reveal my wicked behavior, I am quick to fall before the Lord for mercy. It takes far more courage, however, to stand then before my wounded friend and confess to my relational crimes. Dietrich Bonhoeffer said, "There is no truth toward Jesus without truth toward man. Untruthfulness destroys fellowship, but truth cuts false fellowship to pieces and establishes genuine brotherhood."[1] As we honestly examine our part in a conflict, God's grace will be the salve that helps the wound heal.

Resolve the Conflict. The pastor of our church when I was in high school taught us the principle of thesis, antithesis, synthesis. When you have listened, *then* spoken, attempt to find common ground from which to build a solution. Sometimes a cool-down period may be necessary. But if at all possible, it is wise not to let the sun go down on your anger (Eph. 4:26). Also, Jim and I have found that if a subject is so hot that we can't trust ourselves to be civil, we will discuss it in a public place, like a food gallery at the mall. That forces us to follow certain rules of engagement, if you will.

Sometimes before a synthesis can be agreed on, the situation will call for an uncomfortable confrontation. When we gather our courage to rightfully confront someone in genuine love, we free them and ourselves to change and enjoy a redemptive relationship. We are given a model for confrontation concerning other believers in Matthew 18:15–20. Jesus instructed us to go and show the person his fault. I will risk stereotyping here and say that as women, we resist this approach, because we want things to stay "nice." But "nice" is sometimes settling for "OK," when God intended "wonderful" for us. Wonderful might be just on the other side of conflict. It requires courage— not courage in ourselves or the other party, but courage to obey and trust God for the results.

Paul and Barnabas are a good example of thesis, antithesis, and synthesis. They decided it was a good time to revisit some of the places they had been on missionary journeys together. Barnabas wanted to bring John Mark, his cousin, with them as they had on occasion before: thesis. Paul, on the other hand, didn't want to bring John Mark, because he had deserted them on a previous trip and had not been faithful to the mission. Paul had to confront Barnabas with his difference of opinion: antithesis. The disagreement caused them to agree to separate, and Paul brought in a new assistant, Silas. I am grateful that this incident was included in the Scripture. We see that even people of strong character who were driven by the gospel had relational conflicts, which they resolved wisely and which quite literally resulted in the expanded growth of the early Christian church: synthesis.

As each individual expresses his or her thoughts on resolution, where the two intersect is the beginning of common ground. From there, by preferring the other person in love, and each desiring harmony, the ideas can be synthesized into an agreement of fellowship.[2]

Seek forgiveness. Ultimately, in instances of conflict, the only person we can control is ourselves. Believing the best in the other person hopes for a mutual desire for peace, but regardless of whether the other person expresses repentance, forgiveness is the necessary path. Releasing a debtor opens the way for reconciliation.

Holding grudges or withholding forgiveness will cost us more than friendship. In the long run, it will take a physical toll. Bitterness sits in our soul and becomes a rust that eats through our most armored interiors. Dr. S. I. McMillan said in his book *None of These Diseases,* "When Jesus said, in Matthew 18:22, to forgive seventy times seven, he was thinking not only for our souls, but of saving our bodies from coronary artery disease, high blood pressure, and many other diseases." Our bodies and emotions are intricately designed and connected. Proverbs 17:22 says that a crushed spirit dries up the bones. That is one of the costs of unforgiveness.

Sadly, instead of being proactive toward forgiveness, we brood and nurse our wounds. We are faced with the choice to forgive or not. Such a master of disguise is this imp of unforgiveness. We are fooled into believing we have the upper hand when we withhold forgiveness, and we feel empowered. This false sense of empowerment will cause us to nurse grudges sometimes until the grave. Dr. McMillan said that on many a death certificate the cause of death might well be stated as "grudgitis."

When Peter asked Jesus how many times we are to forgive and boldly said "seven," he thought he was being generous. The Jewish law, the Talmud, said that the requirement was to forgive three times. So when Jesus replied, "Seventy times seven" he was making a poignant point that there is no rule that can govern or limit the supply of forgiveness. A side note here is that he didn't tell us to "forgive and forget." That is a case of a catchy phrase that sounds like it should be in the Bible but isn't. Only God has the capacity to forgive *and* forget. He does, however, pattern forgiveness for us, and then expect us to follow. The entire Bible is a story of forgiveness. The redemption story is of a broken relationship where the One offended goes to the ends of the earth to forgive the offender.

The longer the clutter of unforgiveness sits in our souls, the more life it will consume. I believe that forgiveness is a bedrock of emotional well-being. I was recently in my doctor's office, and he told me that he had seen a record number of "angry depressions" this year. That put me in pause for a few days. When we find ourselves caught between forgiving and not forgiving, we develop an angry crust around our emotions. I think this is why so many women in midlife are being treated for depression. We have lived long enough to accumulate a debilitating collection of unforgiven situations, and one of the collective results is depression.

In my most vulnerable times, I will sit staring off into the day and find that I do some relational accounting. I gather outstanding invoices of unfair hurts and offenses that may go back years. As I relive situations where others have wounded me and truly cost me part of myself, I fight between the knowledge that I should consider these debts canceled and the undefinable need to mark them unpaid. Even as I write these words, my heart pulls me to unfinished business in certain relationships. When an offending person's face is brought to my mind, my stomach tenses. And I know I must surrender again, and I want to want to forgive. But what I'd rather do is curl up in a blanket and go to sleep, and then wake up to discover it's all OK. That's when we truly need God's precious prescription for a healthy, uncluttered soul. Praying for God first to help us see the specific areas we need to forgive in, and then in his grace to give us the courage to follow through, is the recipe for the healing broth of forgiveness.

SIMPLE SUMMARY

In the fall, leaves that have turned pumpkin orange and apple red release their hold on tree branches that have been their home and drift to the earth's floor. They lie scattered randomly until an afternoon wind passes over them, and they collect in a heap at the nearest barrier to their flight. As we grow up and leave our own "home branches" and enter the culture as individuals, as we face our first challenging wind, we collect ourselves in community and face the barriers in our lives with the comfort of relationship.

What is the joy of a celebration without someone to share it with? And aren't tears twice as cleansing when shed in the presence of a good friend? Relationships intensify the experiences of life. They help bear our burdens (Gal. 6:2), and as three young Jewish men showed to a self-consumed king (Dan. 3), they give us courage and solidarity as we reject the false gods of our day and give honor to the true and living God. This is relationship at its finest. It brings out the best in each and strengthens our walk with God.

So far, that's a nice, uncluttered picture. But we know the truth. Even in the first relationship, Adam argued with God because Eve had argued with the serpent, and what resulted was a conflict so vast that it would ultimately cost the very Son of God a humiliating death on the cross. And the clutter collected so high in the garden that the couple had to move out.

Relational conflict is inevitable, and it leaves its marks on us. It is like a scar. A wound is inflicted, and fibrous connective tissue forms at the site of the injury. And while scar tissue may replace injured skin and fade to be almost unnoticeable in time, it remains dense and thick and poorly supplied with blood. It has less pigment and no sweat, oil, or hair glands, leaving it vulnerable to the elements. Intensive scarring may even limit range of movement. The body has forgiven the wound, but it will never totally be the same as before.

Because relational wounds are inevitable, we must brush up on our first aid skills. Conflict wounds our souls. If dealt with, it will only leave a scar, which in time may be almost unnoticeable. The positive side of scarring is that while the damaged tissue grows back with new vulnerabilities, it also grows back tougher than the old skin. If the wound is cared for and healed properly, in time, the resulting scar tissue will become the strongest skin on your body. Conflict can have the same result. While it can leave its mark, if we apply relational first aid and selflessly attempt to restore the fellowship, God's healing touch can redeem the relationship and make it even stronger than before.

Sometimes the conflict we face will be severe and life changing; sometimes it will cost us a little bit of scarring, and sometimes it is just a difference of opinion where neither party is wrong. Whatever it is, we have seen Christ model for us the extent to which we should go to restore fellowship. When we are truly captured by this, the pride we swallow or the scars we wear become mere acts of love and medals of honor as we attempt to reflect his image.

The Three in One who formed us from the mud of the earth and gave breath to us also gave us this soul that longs to be in community. He then places us within reach of one another, where we form connections of friends, mentors, and acquaintances. Within this context, we live out our intended design.

6

PERSEVERING
IN THE EVERYDAY

My youth is like a communion wafer on my tongue—the incarnation of something unforgettable but translucent, spent too soon. I was guilty of believing in Santa Claus, the Easter bunny, and the tooth fairy. My pockets full of wishes, my fists clenching dreams, I walked through childhood with a wonder-filled expression of hope and expectation.

I wished on stars, waved at cabooses, and picked up shiny copper pennies. I imagined the rain was thousands of pearls falling from the angels' necklaces and, in tangled hair and worn corduroy, my lips collected those pearls. There was magic in every day and potential in every thing. I don't remember complaining often about being bored, because, frankly, there was just so much to do. From the mysteries to be discovered in the willow tree-covered backyard in Arlington, to the training of undiscovered circus frogs in Charleston, to the claiming of secret planets for myself in the woods of Alexandria, my to-do list was extensive.

The muse was present. Imagination and wonder mixed to produce a flavorful mixture of awe. Life was big, but not too big for me to get my dirt-stained little hands on it. While now some days the rain just seems like water, if I am careful and still enough, I can still see the faint likeness of a pearl in the drops on my windows. As I scrounge the days for any semblance of that childhood astonishment with the ordinary, I try to see miracles instead of good luck, recognize the presence of holiness or burning bushes, love without fear, and basically just pay attention. A few more years of living have forced me further from the womb, and the view hasn't always possessed the rose hue of my childhood. But on the mornings when I lie crumpled in a heap at my own deficiencies or disappointments or the inequities of humanity, I walk the invisible line between nobility and frailty, between arrogance and whimpering, between child and woman. And when the sun hits the edge of a shiny copper penny, I'm not so numb as to pass it by.

When did we begin to pass by the ineffable without so much as a pause in our pace? When did our next breath become something expected instead of the miracle gift of God's grace? The fact is that in the reality of the kingdom of heaven, the ordinary is extraordinary. But our callous souls have grown hard to the mysteries of life. When I was five, my uncle George could amaze me by pulling a quarter out of my ear. When I was fifteen, I was uninterested in his bogus trick or the insignificant twenty-five cents. At forty, I am in awe of his precious attempts at pleasing me. Wonder and awe come in many forms; it's just more in the seeing than the getting.

We need to help equip our souls to persevere. In the everyday of our souls, we encounter waiting, dealing with the unexpected, disappointment, feelings of insignificance, insecurity, burnout, anger. We need to create simple rites that will help us "see" in new ways and help our souls persevere. As we begin to see again with the wonder of a child, we simplify the complicated realm of soul. The emotional complexities that blocked our view simply untangle into a quieting sense of awe. By creating some sacraments of simplicity, we will imbue the everyday with significance, create symbolic gestures to honor life, and do things that will excite *wonder*.

A still-life painting is one of small inanimate objects, typically everyday items like fruit, flowers, jars, books, glasses, gloves, and so forth. There were, in fact, entire eras of still-life painting dedicated to specific subjects like kitchen items or nature. The painter took time to study and master the intricacies of insignificant items. Post-impressionist painter Paul Cezanne favored still-lifes, but in his *Still Life with Flower Holder* or Vincent Van Gogh's famous still-life of twelve sunflowers in a vase, the everyday items take on a far more honored status. The formality of the arrangement and central placement of the items says, "These things are important." While they are supposed to look like a snapshot of everyday life, it is clear that the artist has taken great care to place each item in such relationship as to highlight its importance. The white napkin, bowl, and pitcher in Cezanne's painting stand out because the rest of the painting is in a dark palette. We suddenly see them as more than pottery and fabric. They seem precious. Van Gogh's sunflowers bend and reach with such personality that they seem more like a portrait. The flowers take on the importance of life. A key element in still-life paintings is what is called "white space." Not literally white, this is the space surrounding the subject. The more of it there is, the more important the subject seems. It creates a quiet, almost reverent scene. It helps excite wonder about the everyday object.

We need white space in our lives if we are to appreciate the everyday. I want to suggest four sacraments of simplicity to help us persevere in the everyday issues of our soul. They will nurture our souls and create the white space necessary for restoring a sense of wonder. They are: (1) solitude, (2) authenticity, (3) gratitude, and (4) celebration.

SOLITUDE

Since my earliest remembrance, I have been drawn to the water. My father might say it was inherited, as his own draw to the water led him into a twenty-six-year career in the navy. Baptism service, bathtub, swimming pool—they were all places I liked to be. When I was in church and someone was being baptized, I would sit up on the edge of my seat, sometimes propped precariously on top of stacked hymnals, so I could attentively watch for the new creature to surface. The calming murals painted behind baptismals of Jesus baptizing people in the Sea of Galilee, the light focused on him, and the dove fluttering above the whole scene transported me. I would repeat this scene many times in my bath, finally satisfied that most of my dolls had been sufficiently "dunked."

Aside from the many symbols water stands for, it is the insulating quality that draws me most. When I am swimming—and I can swim laps until I lose track of time—the weightlessness allows me to move through the water without thinking of my own body. Without that distraction, I become more aware of my interior thoughts. The rhythmic sound of gulps for air and the exhaling of that air, lull me into a sweet and sacred time of solitude. The uninterrupted time becomes a time of listening for the voice of God and gently responding. But just when I am quieting all exterior, tuning into interior, the temptation to begin to "fix" mentally all that is bothering me sneaks through with my next breath. It is highly predictable. It reaches for me around my tenth or twelfth lap. And no matter how many times it has happened, I am caught by surprise, the quiet is interrupted, and I must determine all over again for solitude.

I love the way Henri Nouwen described solitude. He said it is the place of the great struggle and the great encounter. In solitude, the ills of our own heart are diagnosed and the seeds of wholeness are planted. Just before he began his public ministry, Jesus was led by the Spirit (Matt. 4:1–11) into the desert. In this time of solitude, Jesus was tempted with distractions of the physical, flirtations of the soul, and distortions of the spiritual. But it was in the same desert that he exposed the enemy and his strategy and taught us how to stand in the face of temptation. And at the end of this great struggle, he encountered God's provision in the form of angels attending him.

The desert is used synonymously with solitude in much literature of the faith. It symbolizes the reduction of distraction and the amplifying of our need. The dry desert makes us thirsty. In the quiet of solitude, we are reacquainted with our thirst for God. It is not difficult to see the analogy. When Jim and I have been on missions trips to Mexico, by two in the afternoon the dust and the direct sunlight have reduced the distractions of life and placed a simple vision in my mind of water. When we cross back over the border into Texas, we stop at the first food-mart and the selection of soda, fruit drinks, and flavored ice drinks no longer hold the same enticement as they did before we spent hours in the dust and sun. A simple bottle of water is the only thing that will satisfy.

Solitude is not so much a literal place or desert, but, as Andrew Murray said, "The secrecy of the inner chamber and the closed door, the entire separation from all around us, is an image of, and so a help to that inner spiritual sanctuary, the secret of God's tabernacle, within the veil, where our spirit truly comes into contact with the Invisible One."[1] Solitude can be the first minute of the morning, when you are shuffling from bedroom to kitchen to begin the coffee. Or it can be the quiet drive to work, or the silence of folding laundry, or the solo time in the garden. It is anywhere, anytime you can pause and lock out the distractions that drain your soul. It can be that afternoon at the museum by yourself when you wander and enjoy the art, and in the quiet of the museum, you commune with the presence of God. It can be when you sit in a favorite chair with a favorite teacup by the fireplace and watch the fire burn until it's nothing but white-hot coals, and you nurture your soul. When nothing else will work, I find a late-night, quiet, warm tub of wonderful smelling water with a dozen candles will quiet my soul. If the description of solitude sounds more like luxury time to you, you must reorder your priorities and place solitude higher.

The distraction of words—on the television, on the radio, in magazines, in conversation, and my own voice—fills my universe to the point of over-stimulation. Have you ever been out to dinner with a few friends and begun to feel like you were just shutting down, one neuron at a time? With the background noise of people at other tables, the few conversations at your table, the music playing, the menu screaming out options, and the servers asking if they can help you, you are tempted to say, "Yes, carry me to a quiet closet please." Your soul is telling you it needs solitude. We can only take in and give out for so long before we must come away for awhile. Jesus sought out solitude and often withdrew from the frenzy of his world (Matt. 14:13–14, 23–24; Luke 4:42; 5:16). This is enough of a model for me to know it is OK to long for solitary times.

In all of this, we are not talking about a time of emptying ourselves in the eastern tradition, but of quieting ourselves to refill our already drained souls. In many ways, solitude is the alliance of soul and spirit, when the very breath of God seems so near that it ruffles our hair.

In solitude, the wonder of the everyday is clearer. We see God's provisions with a different eye. They become the object of our thirst instead of the flavorless essence of the everyday that we take for granted. If we are attentive, he will expose the strategy of the enemy in our lives and strengthen us to stand. And we will encounter the Invisible One.

AUTHENTICITY

It is May, and I am in the dressing room with nine bathing suits, ranging in size from six to twelve, and covering the stylistic ground from "house-frau" to "indecent exposure." I have continued to exercise all winter and have only allowed a slight bulking-up to combat the "frigid" temperatures of middle Tennessee. But after several months of hibernation in heavy sweaters and wool trousers, my body stands in a state of semishock in front of the full-length mirror in the fluorescent-lit, three-by-three dressing room. My five-foot eight, 127-pound body consumes all of the visible space and reflects an eerie glowing chalk-white covering of skin, broken up by a purple collection of flowers on a shiny fabric that sort of covers two critical areas of my body. "Who is that in the mirror?" is the question I am mulling in my brain when the salesperson knocks, enters, stares, and says, "I'll see if I can find some others for you to try."

Seeing ourselves as we really are can be an alarming experience. For some reason, even at forty years old, I expect to see the body I wore at nineteen reflected back at me in the mirror. It was a good and faithful body that served me well, but somewhere in the past twenty years, waif became woman, and my skin began to conform to a slightly altered shape. The secret is in becoming acquainted with the body I am now walking in and learning to dress it based on its own strengths and flaws. There is truly nothing wrong with wearing the body of a woman who has lived a few years on this planet and bears the badges of courage on her body with pride. Gray hairs, "relaxed" collections of soft flesh, and precious wrinkles that are road maps of our joys and sorrows are all honorable marks of womanhood.

The realities of our bodies are a little easier to recognize. We have the mirror as an honest reflection. But who we are in our souls, our personalities, is a little more elusive. We have fleeting views of ourselves through other people's eyes. We go on thoughtful journeys to "find ourselves"—backpacking, hiking through the wilderness, and pushing our comfort levels to the limit. We trace our lineage and our geographical heritage, trying to put some shape on who we are. And then, to confuse the whole process, just when we get close to defining who we are, we change.

Authenticity is an essential sacrament of simplicity. It is "being" who we really are. If we don't deal honestly with who we are, we will spend our time "persevering in someone else's everyday," and dwelling on the "used to be's" and "what if's." The wonder we see will be a distorted sense of reality.

When I speak of authenticity, I am speaking of the person at the core of us. I am speaking of what animates and motivates us. What we find here will be helpful as we look into mission statements in the next section, but what we *do* is not the same as who we *are*. Please hear this. We so easily lose the "who we are" in the "what we do." It's a common and lamentable mistake we make when we are identifying ourselves and others. The first time we meet someone, we say, "What do you do?" or "Hi, I'm so and so, and I'm a teacher" or "I'm so and so, and I'm a mom." This is informative, but it will not get at the heart of who someone is. It is shorthand for a definition of who we are. We rely on what we do to tell us who we are because we are a productivity-oriented culture. We don't feel significant unless we have a title and are doing something. The problem with this thinking is that if we hang our identity on what we do, we rely on the trappings of a mere job description to describe the wonderful mystery of who we are. It may be shorthand information, but sometimes it ends up confining us rather than defining us.

Sometimes we don't even give a direct answer to "What do you do?" An even more vague answer is the definition by association: "I'm in education," "I'm with the government," or "I'm in banking." This corporate-identity linking connects us to something grander than ourselves, and we use it because we just don't think we are enough. But how can someone understand the wonder of the drooping branches of a willow tree, hanging like green hair, tossing with the breeze, if I were to describe it only as "a tree"? The unique intricacies of identity get lost when we define ourselves by association.

Sometimes we resort to identifying ourselves solely by our "exterior costumes." I am a five-foot-eight, brunette woman. I live in a restored 1920s cottage, drive a seven-year-old Volvo four-door sedan, and am most comfortable wearing jeans, a great white shirt, and easy-wearing black boots. While this is descriptive, it can be misleading. I am naturally a blonde. I long for the open spaces of a contemporary house; don't resemble the three-piece, briefcase-carrying, young professional in the Volvo commercials; and could be equally comfortable in a black dress and pearls. Who we are gets lost in the imaging and stereotyping of our culture. If we can *decorate* ourselves to look like successful people, then we *are* successful people. When we think of ourselves this way, who we are is built on ever-shifting sand, and we are always subject to running to keep up. And to paraphrase the Red Queen in *Alice and Wonderland*, "The faster I run the behinder I get."

I've heard it said that a woman will wear her hair in the style she wore it in when she felt her most confident and popular. If that was high school, college, or whenever, she resorts to that style again, whether or not it flatters her now, because it reminds her of the confident person she was. It really takes courage to discover who we are *now* and live in the authenticity of the moment. But we are children of "I Am" (Exod. 3:14), not "I Was."

Identifying ourselves by these shorthand methods of communication complicates instead of simplifies our lives, because we create layers and layers of superficial selves and our true selves get buried underneath. I suspect that we do it because we are afraid we will come up short if we dare to be honest with ourselves.

For the common to be transformed and the mysterious "who" of our souls to show herself, we must look at our souls in the mirror of authenticity, exposed and vulnerable in the sometimes unflattering fluorescent light of life, and see who is staring back at us. When we take time in solitude to be quiet, if we are honest before God, he will allow us to begin to see the wonder of who he made us to be. Flaws and inconsistencies, weaknesses and failings, beauty and strengths, uniqueness and courage, he gently leads us in discovery of ourselves. And then, wrapped in his grace, we begin to be free to be. I love that in Frederick Buechner's book, *Wishful Thinking, a Theological ABC,* when you look up "self," it says, "See mystery." There he says that when you conduct the examination into who you are, "you do not solve the mystery, you live the mystery. And you do that not by fully knowing yourself but by fully being yourself."

In another of Buechner's books, a twelfth-century character named Godric struggles with and surrenders to who he is as a Holy Man. In his honestly raw humanity and deep conviction of faith, Godric comes face-to-face with being. He says it is as if his hands were gloves and that other hands than his were in them, and it is those hands that people pursue him for. "It's holiness they hunger for, and if by some mad grace it's mine to give, if I've a holy hand inside my hand to touch them with, I'll touch them day and night. Sweet Christ, what other use are idle hermits for?"[2] That's who we are. That's authenticity. That simplifies our life by way of our soul. That teaches us to "be" in the everyday, and it helps restore mystery and wonder.

GRATITUDE

When I entered my freshman year of college, I entered with the zealous confidence of a successful honor-roll, high school graduate. I had more confidence in my academic abilities than my away-from-home survival skills. I packed my typewriter and popcorn popper and made my way to the third floor of the East dorm and joined the other tadpoles entering the pool of higher learning. Gen. Ed. (General Education) was a required class for all freshmen. A five-credit course taught by a team of professors, it combined everything from English to religion in one overconfidence-crushing experience. Our first composition assignment was to write a "compare and contrast" paper on the subject of our choice. My twelve years of education had never dealt me lower than an "A" in English or writing skills. The experience that deposited me with diploma and scholarship on the doorstep of academia coursed through my veins like a dangerous steroid, filling me with delusions of performing far above average. I wryly composed my five-hundred-word paper entitled "Sunny Days vs. Rainy Days" in a mere two hours, three days before it was due. I put it aside in my head and moved on to the more challenging issue of discovering a friendly table in the cafeteria.

The due date came, and I dropped my paper full of sparkling metaphors in the basket and winked to myself at an easy success. The following week when the graded papers were returned to the 120 or so students in my class, I fumed the fume of a martyred saint, unappreciated for her freely shared gift of words. A low *B!* I was astonished. There was a policy whereby we could resubmit a paper for regrading if we were unsatisfied but had to take the second grade regardless of what it was. Without a humble pause, I requested a new reading and grading. A low *C.* I was literally reduced.

Every tiny percentage point I climbed on each successive paper was gold.

I had begun to expect reward for academic performance so much that I lost perspective on the fact that a *B*—low or high—was a fine grade for a first college paper. The *A* I got for the final grade was the best *A* I ever earned. And gratitude began to sprout in my proud soul.

The obsessive pursuit of perfectionism will either ravage the well-being of our interiors, or it can reduce us to to humble gratitude. Do you expect nothing less than A's of yourself and those around you? Does your life either present you with top marks, or you want to trade it in for another one? Is there no appreciation for less than perfect? The perfectionist's soul is weighed down by the thinking that nothing is ever enough. They bemoan the fact that they are too heavy, instead of being grateful they don't go hungry. They complain about all the weeds in their yard instead of being thankful they don't have a view of cement. Cars, houses, clothes, pleasures, and relationships never measure up enough to be grateful for. And the incessant whining of the perfectionist drowns out the simple voice of gratitude.

Another way we miss out on this sacrament of simplicity is that in our pursuit of the "good life," life passes us by. For years, I pursued a professional goal that I was convinced I could not be happy without achieving. In the process, I mourned the fact that good work did not always equal success, and I felt incomplete with my goal unmet. One day as I was feeling sorry for myself, I realized that the reason I was pursuing this goal was to give myself the freedom to enjoy certain rewards in life. Owning a house and a car, making my own hours, and being creatively fruitful were all the results I longed for. But I had become so obsessed with what I thought were the means to my ends that I missed the fact that I was already living the life I was pursuing. It's like the story of the people whose airplane crashed in the river. In their attempt to save their own lives by swimming to the shore, they almost drowned in the unrelenting current. Finally, one of them gave up and surrendered to certain death in the river, only to discover the bottom was about four feet down and that he could walk to the shore. They were so obsessed with the means of swimming to survive, that they missed the fact that they could simply walk and live. What means in your life are you struggling so hard with that you've failed to surrender to simply walking and living? You may already be living the life you are so in pursuit of, but because you got there a different way than you intended, you've missed it.

It is also possible that we miss this sacrament because we fail to let pain and disappointment inform us of the positive things we have to be grateful for. We don't see that it takes deep valleys to define towering summits. Or that it takes a photographic negative to produce a positive print. Or that darkness accentuates light, the contrast of far defines close, and "no" gives meaning to "yes." In their book *In His Image*, Dr. Paul Brand and Philip Yancey speak of how leprosy patients suffer because they can't feel pain. One man did irreparable damage to his leg when he turned his ankle while he was walking. Because the communication system in his body failed to alert him that he had injured himself, he continued to reinjure the ankle until he lost its use and had to have the leg removed. Where have you become so numb that you no longer can tell pain from joy?

The vain things that charm us are fragile as a spider's skein and won't support the full weight of our souls' everyday needs. If we are to persevere, we must learn the sacrament of gratitude.

Make a conscious effort to be grateful to those you come in contact with—the bus driver, gas station attendant, check-out clerk. All need to be appreciated, too. When you give away what you need, you will begin to discover the joys of the everyday. Before you go to sleep at night, list five things you are grateful for that day—everything from the fact that you are now in bed to the fact that the planets haven't collided with the stars. There is so much in between to notice. As you begin the conscious exercise of being aware of things around you, your sense of gratitude will grow exponentially. The fragile filament of thankfulness in your soul will light your way through darker times.

CELEBRATION

Three hundred and sixty-five days a year, at least a half-dozen times each day, my two mini-schnauzers, Rose and Violet, go outside to sniff the dirt and take care of their personal needs. And every time they come back in the house, there is a frenzy tantamount to the Year of Jubilee.[3] The tail-wagging, barking, and dog-dancing go on until the dog biscuits are delivered. And it happens every time, no matter how long they've been out. It doesn't matter how big the biscuit is either. When we've been running low, I've given each of them a half of a half of a biscuit, and the joy is the same. Unbridled celebration of the moment. Then, as quickly as it came, it is gone, and they hurry off to a favorite sleeping spot.

It's only a biscuit. And they only went outside and then came inside. But my dogs are masters of this sacrament of simplicity. Celebrating simple everyday things comes natural to them.

In an episode of the now-canceled CBS series *Northern Exposure,* the eccentric radio disc jockey-philosopher Chris takes a stab at an art project. He plans to create a catapulting contraption from which to fling a cow. When his friend Ed mentions in conversation that Monty Python had flung a cow already, Chris is deflated. With the cajoling of another townsperson, he picks up his pursuit and discovers that it isn't so much what you fling as it is the "fling" itself.

This simple sacrament of celebrating is much the same. It is not so much about the object of our celebrating as it is the celebrating itself. All of life is a gift from God and worthy of celebration. You see, it's not that going outside and then coming inside is such an important event that it needs to be regarded with fanfare, but that the mere act of celebrating reminds us that we are alive. Our souls are nurtured as we approach our daily lives in search of opportunity to celebrate. If we save up all of our party confetti to memorialize only the most significant occasions, it will grow moldy and spoil. We must spend our celebrations generously and revel in the gift of our next breath.

If we fail to celebrate in the simplicity of our next breath, at least we should celebrate in the significant events of our faith. Among the many feast days the traditional church celebrates, the church calendar sets aside certain Sundays to celebrate Christ's birth, Resurrection, Ascension, and baptism. But even with these days set aside for us to celebrate, they get lost in our church formalities and we fail to truly *celebrate* the wonder of these events. If we were to contemplate these unbelievable moments and truly allow them to touch our souls, there would be some parties and celebrations to rival any Fourth of July, New Year's Eve, or Super Bowl parties.

In the Old Testament, when Samuel and the Israelites were in constant battle with the Philistines, they engaged in one particular fight at Mizpah. And on that day, the Lord thundered against the Philistines, and Samuel and the Israelites subdued them (1 Sam. 7:10–13). To honor the occasion of God's deliverance, Samuel collected stones and set up a memorial. He called it *Ebenezer,* meaning "stone of help" because the Lord had helped them up to that point. Samuel celebrates and praises God for what he has done, without condition on the future. He implies that we don't know what God will do tomorrow, but that in this moment, his mercy has been more than certain, and we should celebrate his help.

Without conditions on the future, we must celebrate the moments. Build some of your own "Ebenezers." Or toast the moment with your morning juice. Or have a party to celebrate the first fireflies of the summer. Celebrate a child completing a task, a husband cleaning out the garage, a perfect cup of tea on the first day of fall, but by all means celebrate. Celebrating the moment not only nurtures our soul into being more aware of the wonder in our everyday lives, but it also reminds us of God's mercy and provision.

SIMPLE SUMMARY

When you are neck deep in the perseverables of your everyday soul, what flotation device will keep you from drowning? You wait in the undefinable bog of mid-life, remembering the girl you were, anticipating the woman you are yet to be. You are buffeted by the unexpected, and you take on disappointment like a leaking boat takes on water. Your sense of significance wonders whether she was lost when she took on her partner's last name, or when "mom" became her first name, and whether a successful day of potty training and casserole assembling will be enough to sustain her. The edge seems all too close, and your wings creak at the thought of having to manage a flight over the abyss of emotions.

Sitting beside the lake in Chautauqua, New York, I imagine that my eyes have the magnification capabilities of a fine microscope. If I could see deep into the lake water I collect in my hand, I would be able to see an alliance between fungus and algae. While each of these organisms is fully functional on its own, when they form an alliance, they benefit in ways they couldn't on their own. Like these lichens, wonder and my soul enjoy a symbiotic relationship.

Be still my soul. And wait. Wait in the solitary place. And when you leave the solitary place, take "being" instead of "knowing" for your resolve. As you are grateful for the generosity of the moment, raise your colors and celebrate. And as you do, a sense of wonder will attach itself, and you will persevere.

7

FOCUSING ON
THE GOAL

I can't help but wonder if my majoring in art in college was in any way influenced by the fact that in the year of my birth, 1958, Crayola crayons introduced their perennial favorite sixty-four-color box with built-in sharpener. Binney & Smith, the makers of these child pleasers, began in industrial products, providing the black pigment for the Goodrich Tire Company's manufacture of their first black tires. The pigment not only turned the white tires black, but it made them five times as strong. Binney & Smith went on to manufacture dustless chalk for the classroom, where they discovered a need for good children's crayons. They rose to the challenge and in the early 1900s, rolled out their first box of eight crayons for a nickel.

Much to my joy, they continued their creative color pursuits. There was nothing so thrilling to my young artistic eyes as a brand-new box of sixty-four crayons. And it was an annual occasion. Every Christmas, I would unwrap a new box, fling the lid back and proceed directly for magenta, yellow-ochre, silver, and gold, bypassing the famously popular but common blue, red, yellow, and green. I would eventually get to them as well, but not until they were some of the only crayons left in the box with a point on them. I enjoyed all the features of those slender paraffin wax and pigment sticks. I colored hard and dark and soft and even. I used pointy tips and even tore paper back and used the broad side of the Crayola to cover large areas. But with so many choices in my sixty-four-box, I felt no need to limit my palette to only a few colors. I would learn, however, many years and many crayons later, that there was strength and wisdom in careful color selection.

My freshman year of art school, in Design 2 class, we were assigned a painting project in which we could use one color, adding only black or white to it. I feared I would be creatively stifled as I fondly remembered my sixty-four box. But this intimate focus on one color opened up a world of subtleties, and I began to discover the nuance of color. Further exercises in color made me aware that when you mix more than three colors together, no matter what they are, you begin to approach a noncolor mush. In fact, the result of all colors mixed together is black, thus defeating the point of combining all of those pigments. While my beloved sixty-four box was a great playground for my earliest creative exploits, experience and observation have proven that careful palette selection, which often consists of less and not more, is crucial to the success of a work.

As we continue to simplify our lives in soul, we will see that in much the same way, careful palette selection is the key. If we don't narrow down what we apply ourselves to in life, we will go about trying to do a little of everything and basically contribute mush when we could add our own unique color.

How do we narrow down our choices when it seems that life is a sixty-four-box? What we are passionate about in life motivates us. We go back to Matthew 6:21 again: "Where your treasure is, there your heart will be also" (NIV). If we follow this same passage down, it says that the eye is the lamp of the body and that if your eyes are good, your whole body will be full of light. If they are bad, your body will be full of darkness. No one can serve two masters. This is a call to simplify our soul, to focus, to serve one master. We must identify what we are passionate about, and then, within a context of commitment to godly character, combine this passion with an understanding of our gifts and talents and form what is referred to as a personal mission statement.

The first time I heard the term *mission statement,* I instantly relegated it to the irrelevant, only-for-businesses pile. Although it is good for businesses,

I discovered that it is also an indispensable personal tool. A well-thought-out and prayed-over mission statement becomes the funnel through which all opportunities and activities must fit, and it simplifies our lives by thinning out our palette, by helping us serve one master.

Stephen Covey states the importance of a personal mission statement this way: "Once you have a sense of mission, you have the essence of your own proactivity. You have the power of a written constitution based on correct principles, against which every decision concerning the most effective use of your time, your talents, and your energies can be effectively measured."[1] Translated: If you will take the time to identify the things you are passionate about and recognize your talents, keeping a commitment to godly character as your primary goal, you can simplify your life. A well-constructed mission statement will give you the window through which to look at life and its opportunities. It will make it easier for you to say "yes" or "no" at the appropriate times. That is motivational.

COMMITMENT TO GODLY CHARACTER

Annie Dillard talks about her epiphany concerning chopping wood in her book *The Writing Life*. She says that after chipping and chunking pieces of wood on a chopping block, it finally came to her to aim for the chopping block, not the piece of wood. If you do, she said, then you will go all the way through the piece to the block. As we set up our mission statements, our personal creeds or constitutions, we must aim for the chopping block. What are our lives built on and how do we efficiently get there? Building our personal mission statement on godly character will cause us to pursue life with that as our ultimate aim.

In essence, a good place to begin is the end. When looking back at your life, what description would you want to read? For example, Alexander Hamilton's epitaph reads: "For the patriot of incorruptible integrity, the soldier of approved valor, the statesman of consummate wisdom; whose talents and virtues will be admired, by grateful posterity, long after this marble shall have mouldered into dust." Oliver Hardy's says: "A genius of comedy, his talent brought joy and laughter to all the world." The nameless wife of

Peter Leslie is remembered by this: "She was! But words are wanting to say what. Think what a wife should be, and she was that." And then there are those who are remembered not so fondly, like a Mr. Owen Moore from London, England: "Gone away owin' more than he could pay." And Rab McBeth from Larne, Ireland, was immortalized this way: "Who died for the want of another breath. (He was hanged.)"[2] The words and thoughts that speak for the dash on our tombstone are the ultimate simple statement defining us and will last for a long time. With this as a perspective, we will want to consider our commitment to godly character before we apply ourselves to anything.

Why is godly character important? Because our lives are the best expression of Christ that some people will see. And even more, because it is our purest form of worship to offer back our lives to God reflecting his image.

As you begin to meditate on what godly character looks like in your life, consider some scriptural references like Galatians 5:22–23, which gives a descriptive list of the fruit of the Spirit. Second Peter 1:5–8 also lists qualities and promises that, when you have them and they are growing in you, will cause you to be productive and effective. The first message Christ delivered in his incarnational visit to our world as recorded in Matthew 5 is known as "the Beatitudes." This poetic and astounding description of "blessed"[3] people is a comprehensive summary of Christian character. Philippians 4:8 is a compact statement of perspective for living by: "Finally, brothers, whatever is true, whatever is noble, whatever is right, whatever is pure, whatever is lovely, whatever is admirable—if anything is excellent or praiseworthy—think about such things" (NIV).

Building a mission statement based on godly character does not limit us to specifically spiritual life-oriented pursuits. It simply reminds us of our ultimate goal of reflecting the image of Christ in *whatever* we pursue. We desperately need godly gardeners, caterers, home schoolers, artists, architects, nurses, engineers, teachers, car-pool chauffeurs—the list is infinitely long. Our mission statement encompasses first who we are and then leads us to more specifics about what we do. Equipping ourselves with the goal of godly character will not just cause us to look and act like "nice" people, but it will also cause us to be unmovably, unassailably happy people.

WHAT ARE YOU PASSIONATE ABOUT?

From our earliest pursuit of achievement, it was obvious that things that we were most passionate about would get our best effort. This is why it is rare to find a student who didn't excel in recess and snack time. Math and science, on the other hand, took a particularly developed taste. As we grow and mature, our passions grow and mature with us. And while it seems that identifying them would be a simple matter, sometimes they are hidden beneath layers of "should" and "ought," and can be lost behind living up to the expectations of others.

I remember the day I made the switch from majoring in math to art. It was my junior year of college. I was studying complex equations and derivatives and still challenging my professor on why two plus two always had to be four. Who decided it would be four and not five? Such philosophical sidetracks had hinted to my professor that I might be better suited to a major in the creative arts. While I was excelling academically, it was never a natural fit. I had surrendered to a false value in my culture that held the sciences above the arts. I was being led by *should* and *ought* instead of identifying my own desire and passion. This was complicated by the fact that I assumed I would please my father more with a difficult and challenging academic pursuit. We sometimes make false assumptions of parents' and others' expectations, not giving them the opportunity to love us and be proud of us for pursuing our passions. I went after my art studies much the same as I did recess and snack time as a child. While I would not say that art was an easy major, I would say that the passion I held toward it made it worth applying myself. Dorothy Sayers said in her book, *The Whimsical Christian,* when speaking about life pursuits, that "true love knows no suffering." By this she meant that when you are doing something you are passionate about, it doesn't feel like "work." And I must say that my father rose to the challenge, and I feel his pride in me in everything I apply myself to.

What you are passionate about you will naturally apply yourself to. Make a list of the things you even think you *might* be passionate about. It can be general or specific. The more you put on the list, the easier it will be to identify a pattern or things that go together. Don't be afraid. Sometimes your passions are right before your eyes, but you can't see them. It's like when day is changing to night and the stars are just beginning to make their appearance for the evening. If I try to look right at them, I can't seem to see them, but if I look a little bit away, I see hundreds of them. Just because I couldn't see them when I looked right at them didn't in any way determine their existence. They were there all along, I just needed a different perspective to see them. This may be the case when identifying your passions. Don't worry about making things line up with jobs or professions. Don't worry about writing down things that make logical sense for life pursuits. Just let yourself spill out what comes to you, and don't edit as you think of them. Later, when you look over your list, some things will resonate more than others, and those will be the things to focus in on.

So few people spend most of their time involved with things they are passionate about. I remember when Jim and I were considering a very distinct career change. We had a meeting together and wrote down all the things we were spending our time on, in order of most to least time spent. Then, in a second column, we wrote down all the things we would like to spend our time on if money or circumstance were not an issue. We discovered that our lists were almost direct opposites. The things we cared about least we were spending the most time on and vice versa. That night we began to make practical plans to change our situation and equip us to pursue the things we were passionate about.

What are you spending the most time on, and does it line up with what you are most passionate about? Examine your heart and try to identify and put into words what you are enthusiastic about. Enthusiasm comes from two root words, *en* and *theos,* meaning, "in God." The dictionary even defines it as "supernatural inspiration." Passion that is God inspired will result in life motivation.

WHAT ARE YOUR GIFTS AND TALENTS?

When my Aunt Gene was teaching daily vacation Bible school one summer, she was privileged to work with the seven- and eight-year-olds. The subject of humility was the lesson one morning, after which the students went out for recreation. When they came back in for class, one of the boys was busting with excitement. Finally he said, "Miss Gene, wasn't I the one who hit that home run that knocked those three runs in?" He so much wanted for her to know what he had done, but the humility lesson was heavy on his mind.

We are much the same way as we try to examine our own lives for gifts and talents. We are afraid that if we honestly identify things we are good at, people will find us to be too self-impressed. Theologian John Stott spoke of the paradox of how Jesus taught about himself while at the same time his behavior was completely unself-centered. He had both the greatest self-esteem and the greatest self-sacrifice: "He said he was going to judge the world, but he washed his apostles' feet." His servant's heart kept his confidence in God's design in perfect balance. This perspective should free us to confidently recognize the talents that God has graciously given us and equip us to become genuine servants.

You might begin by making a list of all of your achievements. Make it as comprehensive as you can. Remember your early school years, recurring achievements, and any successes you enjoyed. Again, a pattern will emerge. And as you begin to write things down, you will become more comfortable with identifying and labeling your talents. You will be able to detach yourself, and they will become factual pieces of information to aid you in your search.

I have kept a file over the years that Jim has laughed at out loud. I realize it sounds a little eccentric. It is labeled "Awards: Kim." In it I have certificates of achievement from as far back as junior high and report cards from as far back as elementary school. The file includes news clippings, cards, ribbons, and awards. If I could get my bowling trophies in there, I would. Jim understands the importance of this file to me, but he still enjoys chortling when our frequent flyer statements come in the mail with a list of the awards available, and he asks if I want to put mine in my awards file. It really isn't a show-off file, but a record of achievements. I even have a small Japanese flag in it that was tied to my hiking stick when I climbed Mount Fuji as a thirteen-year-old. The file is full of little reminders of times when I worked hard and was rewarded. It's fun to look back and see that as early as grade school my teachers picked up on my interest in art and creative writing. And whenever I pull out my recorder to play a song, I remind Jim of my seventh grade "Certificate of Outstanding Achievement on Recorder." Again, he chortles. These were all hints of the passions God had placed deep in my soul that I would eventually discover and pursue. Seeing the trail of evidence confirms my thoughts as an adult.

As you come to the end of the things you can think of, add to your list things that others have affirmed in you. Sometimes they will see things in your life such as talents that you have begun to take for granted. Things we do well and with ease we easily overlook as talents. We think talent always has to be in the context of sweat. Seeing yourself through others' eyes is a good thing in this case. It brings an enlightening perspective.

I remember in my high school youth group that we used to do something called a "love feast." We would get in small groups and everyone would have a blank card for each member of the group. We would write a positive adjective about every person on their card, then give it to them. I took my cards home and looked over them from time to time, and the Lord used the words of my peers to plant affirmations in my heart. Yearbook slogans like "nice," "sweet," and "good smile" were all off limits. You had to think of the person and write an appropriate positive description for them. They were still somewhat general words, but they added to my collection of hints about myself and my talents.

At this point, you may be comfortable enough to write down things that you believe you are good at. You might surprise yourself at how many things you will discover once you get going. Don't leave anything out. Being a good listener, good in an emergency, a good nurturer, good at expressing your thoughts, and having good intuition are as important as talents like sewing, being good with numbers, gardening, painting, teaching, and leadership.

You are a precious resource. If you don't use the gifts and talents you have, they will wither. Jesus cursed the fig tree for not producing fruit (Matt. 21:19). It had all the capabilities, but didn't use them. The One who authored the talents in you intended for you to use them.

WRITING OUT YOUR PERSONAL MISSION STATEMENT

Butter, flour, salt, and sugar are generic ingredients found in many recipes. But combined in the prescribed amounts and baked for twenty-five minutes in a 325-degree oven, they will produce heavenly shortbread cookies, the smell of which is almost as good as the flavor. Likewise, you have assembled the ingredients for your personal mission statement, and now they must be appropriately combined and "cooked" so as to give off the sweet aroma of authentic, intentional living.

It is a fairly easy process of cut and paste. You may want to begin with a phrase like: "In the context of a commitment to godly character." If after reviewing some of the Scripture you feel particularly drawn to a specific quality or two, you might begin with: "I am committed to truth, and honesty. . . . " Or you may want to close your statement with: ". . . through which I desire to express godly character." However you end up saying it, it is important to confess your commitment to reflecting the image of God as you form your life's creed.

Next, you should have two lists, one expressing your desires and passions in life and one expressing your gifts and talents. To be able to synthesize these into a cohesive statement, you must spend time meditating and reflecting on what you have written—"cooking," if you will. In the process of slowly contemplating your lists, time will be faithful, and the Holy Spirit will begin to reveal themes and words that resonate with your soul. The things that you consistently skip over quickly can be crossed off. Eventually, you will be able to cross more and more off. It will be like cleaning out your closet. The first time through, it is easy to identify the deadwood, but it gets harder with each progressive cleaning. Then one day you will find that the red sweater you thought you would never part with seems totally extraneous to you, and you will grab it and toss it. This is how your list will narrow down over time. As you look at what you have written, remind yourself to think in terms of what motivates you over the long term and how you would want to see your life when you looked back over it.

You will find that when you have significantly reduced the lists, the passions and talents that remain will directly relate. Laurie Beth Jones in her book, *The Path,* gives several pages of verbs to help in creating a mission statement.[4] At this point you may want to create an arbitrary list of verbs, either by paging through a dictionary or writing down what comes to your mind. This will be the tool to shorthand your passions and talents. For example: "connect, accomplish, encourage, perform, motivate, support, counsel, pursue. . ." If when you look back over your list of verbs you don't find yours, keep writing.

Jones also gave an example of a woman who initially stated her mission as "to raise a happy family." She pointed out that this covered the woman's family life and no other areas. As well, it made her responsible for the happiness of others, which she ultimately could not control. They rewrote it together to read: "My mission is to create, nurture, and maintain an environment of growth, challenge, and unlimited potential for all those around me." This gave the mission statement life in or out of the home, even after the children were grown. She also told of a woman who worked at a cancer care center who wrote her mission statement as: "To inhale every sunrise and look under every rock for the joy life has to offer." She obviously brought a lot to her patients.

Your mission statement can be as long or as short as you want it to be. However, the more concise it is, the easier it will be to remember and apply. Try to be broad enough to include many facets of your life, but not so general as to dilute the meaning. For example, if your statement was "To succeed at whatever I do," you would want to go back and suggest what "succeed" looks like and list specifics for "whatever."

Someone who narrowed their list down to a passion for education, decorating, and entertaining and their talents to communicating, nurturing, and organizing might say, "I will study and equip myself to produce a nurturing and creatively inspiring environment wherever I am, making reflecting the image of Christ my utmost goal." The words leave room for a variety of specific applications, but narrow the field of focus.

Once you have your personal mission statement in a manageable form, you may want to write it and post it in places you will see it often. But don't carve it into wood, engrave it in metal, or tattoo it on your upper arm. While parts of it may be timeless, most likely it will be the kind of thing that evolves with your life. You will want to reassess from time to time. In the same way that Abraham was faithful to a faithful God, kept his bags packed, and was ready to respond to God's leading, we must not hold on to a mission so tightly as to miss the reality of what is happening in our lives. Abraham's willingness to leave everything behind in order to follow the voice of God challenges my nature. When I finally get a line on what I think I'm supposed to do, I am very stubborn to change. But if Abraham had refused to leave and move from his comfortable home in Ur, a godless city, to Canaan, which became the focal point for much of Israel's history and the rise of Christianity, he would have missed God's promise of blessing on his life. In our stubbornness, we might cling to the comfort of what we know and miss the promise of our future. Your specific mission may change. For a season, it may be clearly one thing, and then the God who led Abraham and who designed the changing seasons may call you to move in a new direction. As you adapt and stay close to the voice that directs, the enchantment of the changing seasons will be a delight.

Writing your mission statement out on paper, however, is a good idea. Post it by the telephone, so that when opportunities come to you via that necessary but often annoying invention of Alexander Graham Bell, you will be reminded of your mission statement before you robotically say "yes." Write it on your calendar to help remind you of what is important to you when scheduling your life. Put it on your mirror, bedside table, in your Bible, and, most of all, in your soul. Pray for God to give you occasion to use your abilities in ways that will express his character in the minutia of the everyday as well as in the grand perhaps.

SIMPLE SUMMARY

I have an inch-and-a-half-tall red rubber Santa, carefully preserved inside of two glued-together, empty, clear McDonald's ketchup containers. A rough hole was jabbed in the corner of the plastic container and an unbent paper clip was slipped through it, adding the functional finishing touch to a treasured Christmas ornament that my niece made for us when she was seven. It isn't that this Santa is particularly special. He is round and has a full sack tossed over his shoulder, and his left arm is extended as if he were hailing a cab. But my niece thought he was too special not to have some sort of frame that separated him from his environment. While at first glance you might think that Santa is trapped inside, on further examination you would come to understand that my little red rubber Santa appears far more precious and special set apart in his plastic world.

If you have found this entire exercise of composing a mission statement to be too rigid and confining, on further examination you will come to understand that our lives are far too precious and special not to have a frame that distinguishes us from our world. Without a personal mission statement we can find ourselves lost and overwhelmed, and our lives will spill out around us with no intentionality. We easily find ourselves reacting to life instead of being proactive. A mission statement is not intended to lock us in to a rigid lifestyle but to give us a framework from which to view life and all of its opportunities. It equips us to separate the distractions from the important.

From the time I could first talk, people have asked me, "What do you want to be when you grow up?" For a very short, confused period in my life, I thought I would be a man. Somehow, I had decided that everyone was a little girl when they were young and that when they finally grew up, they became men. After all, my dad was the oldest person in my life, and I thought that when my older sister, my mother, and I all finally grew up, we would be like Dad. After that got straightened out, I moved on to decide that I would become a preacher, like Pastor Kolb, who baptized me when I was seven. When I told that to this loving and precious Baptist pastor from Memphis, Tennessee, he smiled and probably thought that about as likely as me growing up to become a man. I had short periods of wanting to be a flight attendant, secret agent, lawyer, Miss America in braids, and president. I even remember my dad changing the words to a song being performed in the Macy's Thanksgiving Day Parade we watched on television from "every little boy . . ." to "every little girl can be president." I grew up in a nurturing and encouraging home environment, but I still had to search this question out for myself.

While I have a pretty good grasp on my personal mission statement right now, I didn't eight months ago. And five years before that, I was pretty clear, but four years earlier I was clueless. What I'm getting at is that we can be confident in knowing "who" we are to be as women of God in process, but the "what"—the specifics of our mission statement—is always subject to the season of the Spirit's guiding. I think that God's concern is mostly in the "who," but he has designed and equipped us better as individuals for some things than others.

Having a personal mission statement will help simplify your life. It will give you definition and focus. And it will give you confidence in God's unique design of you. Don't allow uncertainty in the specifics to steal the peace of God's promise for giving you a future. "'I know the plans I have for you,' declares the LORD, 'plans to prosper you and not to harm you, plans to give you hope and a future'" (Jer. 29:11, NIV).

8

SUMMARY OF PART II

Just beneath the translucent layers of skin that clothe us sits more than sixty thousand miles of transport vessels for the life-giving blood that rushes to and from our hearts. Our circulation system sends out oxygenated blood and nutrition and returns with metabolites that must be filtered and excreted. Blood flows from the heart through arteries and returns to it through the venous system. From the aorta, the largest and most important artery in the body, to the capillaries, the smallest of blood vessels, we are supplied with the liquid essence of life. Not only is this a masterfully designed, life sustaining system, but in it we find the code of life, the genetic history of who we are. DNA is a code so distinct and individual that it almost spells our names.

Just inside the skull is a soft, jelly-like structure weighing around three pounds: the brain. It is the housing of our intelligence, learning, memory, and consciousness. It directs movement and emotions. Beneath every square millimeter of the brain's cortical sheet are one hundred thousand neurons, the basic unit of the nervous system. The brain itself consists of ten thousand million neurons. It is the "master computer" of our flesh and bone, and without it we would cease to function.

We were made from very complex mud. And even with the knowledge of our genetic code, DNA, and an understanding of our life fluid, blood, and an identification of our processing and control center, the brain, there still exists the mystery of the soul. It is not identifiable as part of our flesh-and-blood housings, but is an awesome wonder of divine breath. Our understanding of ourselves being far more than mud was placed within us, leaving no trace of its origin but the invisible fingerprint of God. This awareness speaks to us like a burning bush, and we must remove our shoes, for this is holy ground.

If we are to hear the burning bush speak, we must reduce the clutter in our souls. We must initiate and maintain healthy relationships and equip ourselves to handle conflict. When the sting of gossip finds its mark in your heart, don't allow it to grow and fester, but deal with it immediately. Speak the truth in love and pray to understand, then be understood.

The burning bush will speak in our everyday life as we restore wonder. When we nurture our souls with sacraments of simplicity, they help us to participate in the holy mystery. We create white space in our lives which sets the "everyday" apart as special.

The burning bush will direct us as we focus on a personal mission statement. Instead of aimlessly filling our days, we can maximize our passions and talents.

The scientific understanding of our body in no way diminishes the mystery of it. And in that sense, if someone were able to define the soul scientifically, it would not reduce the mystery of it. Science may satisfy its need for understanding, but how would it explain the intricate design without there being a designer? It is in this mysterious soul that we have a need and hunger for love and relationship. It is in the soul that we respond to the ordinary as if it were extraordinary. And it is in our souls that we long for our lives to have purpose and significance. These are not scientifically definable things, but witnesses to humanity's connection to the infinite.

Stand still; the bush is burning.

WORKING IT OUT

1. I have relationships that I need to unclutter.
    (no) 1   2   3   4   5 (yes)
2. Can you identify relationships in your life from each of the seven categories (family, friends, acquaintances, soul mate, mentor, apprentice, and former relationships) listed? Which relationships are lacking in your life? Are there positive steps you can take to change that?
3. Name three people in your life who are emotional assets. Are there people in your life you can identify as emotional drains? Can you foresee a way to change the relationship into an asset? Is it possible that you need to invest less time in some relationships?
4. I manage conflict by:
    *   avoiding it.
    *   bullying it.
    *   giving in.
    *   taking a deep breath and dealing with it.
5. Do you have a plan for dealing with conflict? Where do you get bogged down?
6. If you deal with frequent depression, could it be that you need to forgive someone in your life? Do you have a friend who can help you pray through that unresolved conflict?
7. I take time to nurture my soul.
    (no) 1   2   3   4   5 (yes)
    (Possible reasons for "no": I feel guilty. I'm too busy. I never thought to).
8. Do you have a sense of wonder? Remind yourself to "see" the world around you.
9. What does your ideal "white space" look like?
10. What sacraments of simplicity do you need to institute in your life?
    *   Planned solitude? Silence? If you can't set up a daily time for solitude, plan a weekly time. Consider taking a day of silence—no television, no music, no books, no talking—a few times each year.
    *   Living honest to who you are? Do you define yourself by what

you do instead of who you are? Prepare yourself for when you are introduced to people. Write out an authentic answer to the question "Who are you?"

- Being aware of all you have to be grateful for? Have you recognized the "Grand A-ha"? Each morning this week identify two things in your life that you had missed as the Grand A-ha (for example, the simple joy of going to sleep beside your mate, the unfathomable greatness in the design of your eye so that you can see stars at night, the assurance of prayers divinely listened to, and so forth). You may want to keep a Grand A-ha journal, or post notes around your office or car.

- Celebrating life? Create some of your own Ebenezers. Pile some rocks at the edge of your driveway to remind you to celebrate God's faithfulness. Color hard-boiled eggs to eat Monday morning to celebrate the beginning of the week, drink orange juice in stemmed glasses to toast the morning, or celebrate a personal victory with a "bring your favorite ice cream" party, or celebrate a week of faithful exercising with a gift to yourself from your favorite store.

11. Commit to spending time creating a personal mission statement. Spend time meditating on what godly character should look like in your life specifically. Write out your passions and your talents. Ask other people to help you identify what your strengths are. Ask God to direct your path (Prov. 16:9; Jer. 29:11). Plan to reassess at least once a year.

12. There is a tradition in a Brethren in Christ church where they come to bring what is heavy on their souls to God. They sit assured they are in the presence of him who is able, and lay their hands out in front of them, palms up. They imagine that they are holding before him what is not well with their souls, and in a sign of surrender, when they have laid it down, they turn their palms to the ground, symbolizing that they hold it no longer. What is not well with your soul? Bring it before the loving God who will meet you in your need.

Prayer: Oh God, help me simplify my soul. May I see those around me whom I can be in rich relationship with, loving boldly, serving efficiently, tearing down divisions and building community as far as I can effectively reach. Bless my efforts at soul nurturing and restoring wonder. Help me identify the talents you have generously built into me and match them with the desires you've planted in my redeemed heart. And I will be in awe of the mystery of your touch that gives me soul.

SOUL: AT A GLANCE

- You are more than mud.
- Reduce the clutter. Manage conflict in relationships. We all have at least seven categories of relationships. To manage conflict, identify it and have a plan to deal with it.
- Persevere in the everyday. Restore a sense of wonder with sacraments of simplicity: solitude, authenticity, gratitude, and celebration.
- Focus on the goal. Create a personal mission statement. Combine your passion with your talent in the context of a commitment to godly character.

PART III.

SPIRIT:
SIMPLICITY
IN OUR
SPIRITUAL WORLD

"Superficiality is the curse of our age. The doctrine
of instant satisfaction is a primary spiritual
problem. The desperate need today is not for a
greater number of intelligent people, or gifted
people, but for deep people."
—Richard J. Foster

"To have a spiritual life is to have a life that is
spiritual in all its wholeness—a life in which the
actions of the body are holy because of the soul,
and the soul is holy because of God dwelling and
acting in it."
—Thomas Merton

There is a gothic devotion to routine. Its rhythm secures my feet to the ground. It is Friday. Shirt day. White shirt laundry day. Big Mary begins the weekly rites.

In our family there was Aunt Mary, my cousin Little Mary, and Big Mary. Big Mary worked for my aunt and uncle at the house on Sherwood Road in Little Rock, Arkansas, through most of my elementary school years. She was a loving part of the family and respected and needed by all of us. When I was four, she taught me that neither age nor skin color were barriers to friendship. We went to live at the house on Sherwood when my Navy Dad was stationed on an ice-breaker at the South Pole. My Mom wanted us girls to be near family. My aunt and uncle had raised all of their children to adulthood and had a five-bedroom house, only one of which was occupied. They graciously took us in. Not just into their house, but into their home.

We moved in, and somehow my mother and her thirteen- and four-year-old daughters were lovingly incorporated into the family routine. I sat faithfully in front of the console black-and-white for *Captain Kangaroo* in the mornings while my aunt (the nurse) and my uncle (the doctor) went to the hospital to work, and my mom, dressed in a *I Love Lucy* car coat and Wicked-Witch-of-the-North pointy, black, high-heeled, fur-lined ankle boots, drove my sister to junior high school. Big Mary would make me a breakfast of egg-in-the-hole. After that, there were cabinets full of silver to be polished, linens to be ironed, floors to be scrubbed and waxed, and on Fridays, there were white shirts to be laundered.

I carried the bag. We started the search in my uncle's room, and I was Big Mary's assistant. She graciously made me feel like an integral part of the process, rather than an annoying four-year-old, and she taught me that neither age nor the color of your skin is a barrier to friendship. As if on a cattle drive, we had to herd the shirts from closets, armoires, under beds, on the doors, behind the doors, on the bathroom floor. They were hiding, always hiding. You see, they did not want to be made clean.

I understand. I don't go willingly either. But there was no escape from Big Mary's trained professional eye. One by one, we collected and firmly encouraged the white shirts into the bag, which was at this point slung across her large, round, womanly form. They would try to jump for freedom, but she would quickly close the bag, sealing their Friday fates. Once they were secured, we marched them to the garage, where the washer and dryer sat at the ready. This walk was so ominous to me. The downstairs of a two-story building/garage was dark and damp, and I was convinced it housed all of my childhood monsters. Big Mary understood my apprehensions and would extend her large fleshy palm and swallow my tiny vulnerable hand in the safety of hers. Then she would crack a smile at me and say, "Child, there's no monsters out there. They're all upstairs under your bed."

Then the real work began. She fought with them. One big knee up on one oxford cloth arm. A tireless struggle against neck and wrist grime. A mysterious poultice of detergent, bleach, and spit. Scrub. Whine. Wet fingers, crimson knuckles. Finally, sweat on her forehead, she would force them one at a time unwillingly into the washing machine, where they were beat senseless for twenty minutes. When the wash, rinse, repeat finally stopped, we opened the lid confidently and pulled the shirts out. They were limp, the fight gone out of them. They had surrendered. We could safely assemble them as a group in the wicker basket and carry them to the clothesline in the backyard. And Big Mary would pin them up, one arm east and one arm west, and they would hang in the afternoon breeze and be made clean and fresh for a new week.

I do not like the process of being made clean. And being made clean sometimes means facing my monsters. But a large hand extends and swallows my tiny hand and says, "Come along. It's not safe, but it's good."[1] Then, finally, we are gathered up with much sweating and whining, and we surrender to discover that a long time ago one arm was pinned east and one arm was pinned west on our behalf that we might be made clean for a new life.

And this is the simplicity of the truth of the spirit: that we were not clean but that the Father saw us through loving eyes, and by the gift of his unlimited love in the form of Jesus, we were made clean. It is in the largeness of this one gift that real life begins. After that, it is a lifetime of becoming. We must be reminded that we are in a marathon, not a sprint, that we are pilgrims on a long journey, not tourists with a passing interest in the spiritual life.[2] It is here that we begin to simplify in spirit by becoming clean, and then by being pilgrims who have habits of holiness, and mostly by having hearts wholly after God.

9

REDUCING THE
CLUTTER

In Madeleine L'Engle's book, *The Love Letters,* her character described how applejack is made. After apples are harvested, the flesh is juiced. This creates the essence. Apple juice is left outside all winter in a keg. It freezes, but not all of it. The small core of purest liquid inside does not freeze. That is what applejack is made of, the *pure* essence.

Before sophisticated technology, gold was purified by the goldsmith heating the fire beneath the vat that held the complex ore. As the mixture was heated, the impurities would rise to the surface. The refiner would remove the dross and repeat the process until when he looked down into the vat, he could see his image clearly reflected in the pure gold.

I want to be reduced to pure essence. The things in my life that are unpure must be identified and eliminated. When the heat is turned up in my life and circumstances are intense, or when life seems cold and unbearably bleak, my sin is made evident. My generous Heavenly Father makes it possible for me to relieve my heart of its dross. As I avail myself of this opportunity for confession, I am being reduced, and the image of Christ is more easily seen in my life. And I am called into holiness one more time as the regenerating art of grace is performed.

The Voice says, "If you will confess your sins, I will forgive, forget. Go and sin no more" (1 John 1:9; Isa. 43:25; Heb. 8:12; John 8:11).

There is no more lethal clutter than the clutter that collects in our spiritual lives. The precious luminous place within us that speaks for our spirit shows dirt like a white silk blouse. A casual caustic remark that reduces a nonpresent friend, the pride-filled eyes that dress down the simple, the idol worship of acquiring things at the expense of pure character, contributing to the celebrity addiction of our culture by preferring someone over another because of their status, allowing ourselves to be defined by what we do and have instead of who we are, being deaf to the neediest among us, and choosing self over God; sin is toxic to any attempt at reflecting the image of Christ.

If we are to unclutter our spiritual houses and simplify our lives, we must have clean hearts. The tools we will need to perform this spiritual house cleaning are to: (1) identify the plumb line, (2) give a good confession, and (3) receive forgiveness.

IDENTIFYING THE PLUMB LINE

I remember the first time I hung a shelf on the plaster walls of our 1920s cottage. Being a one-time math major and the daughter of a man who would wear a fully equipped tool belt—and make use of all of those tools—and measure five ways to hang one picture, I was on the cusp of a major project. I gazed into our meagerly equipped orange tool box with removable tray that my dad had given us for Christmas, selected a hammer, three molly bolts, one retractable twelve-foot tape measure, and a number two pencil as my assisting devices. I decided where I wanted the bottom of the shelf to hang: thirty-two inches from our nine-foot ceiling. The shelf was twenty-four inches wide so I marked where I wanted the end to be. Then I proceeded to measure thirty-two inches from the ceiling at one-foot intervals until I reached twenty-four inches. Next, I connected the dots with my number two pencil. I mounted the shelf supports with the molly bolts across that line, and then with much anticipation I placed the shelf on the supports. My project resulted in a shelf that had a very distinct starboard list. Instead of creating a plumb line with a level based on a dot thirty-two inches from the ceiling, I hung the shelf relative to the unpredictable plaster ceiling of a house that had been settling for more than seventy years.

When we consider right and wrong, we must begin by identifying the plumb line. The historical influences of the Renaissance, the Enlightenment, the Industrial Age, and Darwinism have resulted in two models of truth. In one model, truth is defined by God for everyone, and it is objective. In the other, truth is defined by the individual and is subjective.[1] The first model gives us the plumb line for our behavior, whereas the second model, subjective truth, results in relative morals and behavior with a "distinct list" to it.

Our culture would have us believe that recognizing a plumb line or an ultimate guide for our interior moral compass is a narrow lifeview. But as Christians, not only do we believe in objective truth that God has revealed through Scripture, we believe an understanding of right and wrong has been instilled in each human being. The logic of a subjective belief system that says there is no right or wrong is not born out when we consider that in almost any culture in the world acts of murder, selfishness, stealing, and adultery are universally recognized as wrong. And if there are universally understood rights and wrongs—objective truth—where did this sense of conscience come from?

The word *conscience* originates from two words meaning to "know with someone." Our God-installed conscience is the silent discerning of our thoughts, words, motives, and actions in concert with the Holy Spirit. "With the Holy Spirit" is the essential in this process of discernment. It may sound mysterious, but it is the combination of the mysteries of the Spirit and the verities of the Bible that moves on our conscience and urges us toward truth.

In our culture, the conscience has become seared over on the altar of the individual. I remember the day I realized that when given the choice to do the right thing, people, including Christians, do not always do it. That day, in the middle of my third decade of life, any remaining flicker of innocence I held was snuffed out. I don't want to give the wrong impression here. I am as dirty a sinner as anyone, but I know how to be nice. Obviously, "being nice" falls several stories below holiness. But I thought that at least to avoid embarrassment, people could be counted on to do the right thing, to be nice. The problem is, with situational truth, the definition of "the right thing" is floating and unpredictable and becomes subject to the best interests of the individual.

The most confusing is the Christian who by definition believes in objective truth but who in actuality lives by subjective truth. When we allow ourselves to pollute our convictions about things the Scripture has spoken clearly on, we clutter our spirits, and slowly the pure essence begins to resemble our own face more than the image of Christ. It is only with the help of the Holy Spirit that we can learn to discern right from wrong. And it is only with the power of the Holy Spirit that we can choose to do right.

Admitting our faults and our culpability is not natural. We have resisted being told right from wrong since childhood. On any school playground you can hear a conversation that goes, "You aren't the boss of me," or "You can't tell me what to do," or "You aren't my mom or dad," or "You aren't the teacher." While we recognize authority figures and their judicial roles, given the slightest taste of independence, our breath begins to reek of the scent of forbidden fruit, original sin, and our desire to become our own gods.

It is in the context of this desire that sin is given birth. We choose to ignore the Spirit guiding us in our interiors, identifying right and wrong, and serve ourselves a healthy portion of "me." The layers of guilt and lies we then create do anything but simplify our lives.

But, somehow, the Father still hears our voice in honest confession and is generous with grace that responds in forgiving and forgetting.

A GOOD CONFESSION

All of our sins were forgiven and our salvation secured when Christ died on the cross. The opportunity for ongoing confession will not earn us anything, but it can release us from the baggage of shame and regret.

Richard Foster, in *Celebration of Discipline,*[2] quoted St. Alphonsus Liguori, saying, "For a good confession three things are necessary: an examination of conscience (which will reveal specific sins, not just general), sorrow, and a determination to avoid sin." We will look at: (1) an honest examination of our conscience, (2) a godly sorrow for our sins, and (3) repentance.

As the Holy Spirit leads us in an *honest examination of our conscience,* we will discover clutter. Sometimes it will be hard to look at and we will shrink back from seeing, or we will wrestle with the Spirit. The deeper the impurity, the hotter the flame will feel. There have been times when the ugliness of my self has caused me literally to squeeze my eyes shut in shame. At that moment, I am vulnerable. I can walk away and relieve the pain for a moment, or stay with it and begin to identify my sin by name as I prepare for confession. If we will to change, the Holy Spirit leads us from the safety of our perceived self and brings us to see our true selves as sinners who sin.

We will want to reduce the gravity of our sin by referring to it in vague and inconsequential language. I remember being required to read Dr. Karl Meninger's book *Whatever Became of Sin?* my freshman year of college. And as I speed-read through this one of many books that so strained my eyes that semester that I had to wear a patch, I was confronted with the thought that sin had become innocuously relegated to "inappropriate" or "unfortunate" behavior. The sting was missing.

Eugene Peterson warned about the dangers of "selfism and sappy substitutes for the steel imperatives of Jesus. . . . We need rigorous and detailed schooling in the nuances of temptation, the ways of the devil, and our seemingly endless capacity for deceiving ourselves and being deceived."[3]

When we use terms that excuse or justify our actions instead of owning up to the ugliness that is ours, we cheapen the significance of the cross. What caused the life to be drained out of the Son of God was not an "oops" or a "little mistake" but our inexhaustible capacity for wretchedness. In a culture that winks at sin, *conscience* and *virtue* become irrelevant terms. C. S. Lewis said, "What we call asking God's forgiveness very often really consists in asking God to accept our excuses . . . What we have got to take to him is the inexcusable bit, the sin."

In defining *sin*, I would like to expand our thinking beyond the elementary no-no's that we have all heard. Not to excuse any sin, but our heart attitudes are far more corrupt and subversive than our clothing, food, drink, and the vocabulary we use when we drive alone. Susanna Wesley, the mother of nineteen children, one of them John Wesley, the "father" of Methodism, gave this definition of *sin:* "Whatever weakens your reason, impairs the tenderness of your conscience, obscures your sense of God, and takes off the relish of spiritual things—that to you is sin." We have no time for foolishness. Knowing God is a full-heart commitment, and anything we pursue more can become sin and collect like clutter in our spirits.

Augustine, who wrestled deeply with his own sins, said, "We are restless until we find our rest in God alone." Have you been trying to find your rest in an inadequate impostor?

Simone Weil, a woman of faith from early in the century, as a sign of solidarity with the beleaguered French Resistance troops, refused to have any sugar as a young girl if the troops had none. Her statement on sin was: "All sins are attempts to fill voids." And the brilliant mathematician, scientist, philosopher Blaise Pascal said that we carry a "God-shaped vacuum inside of us." Our attempt at filling the void with anything other than God is the source of sin.

The original sin that took place in paradise was ultimately an example of filling the void with the wrong thing. Eve was tempted by the speaking serpent to distort God's good intention of forbidding them to eat the fruit from a specific tree as a restriction on her personal rights. Then this master manipulator planted seeds of unbelief and pride: "You won't really die. God was just trying to keep you from knowing what he knows." While she had freedom to select from the entire garden to fill her desires, Eve fell to the temptation to steal the one thing she didn't have to fill herself with. You can easily see the next step in the deception, and Eve's rationalizing that sin was necessary for her to evolve in her knowledge.

It seems that the serpent continues to speak in familiar manipulations of the truth. Prison Fellowship reported on a symposium called "The Evolution of Deception."[4] It was proposed that deception and evil are necessary adaptations for evolution. They gave the example of a species of firefly whose hungry males have perfected the art of deception. Rather than hunt their own food, they mimic the signature flash of the female and lure potential mates. The unsuspecting suitor becomes dinner before he can discover that "she" was a "he." Another example in support of their hypothesis was of an African beetle which also uses deception to get his dinner. By sticking ants to its body, it impersonates ants to get into the colony and dine on the inhabitants. Prison Fellowship goes on to caution that it isn't a far leap from the symposium's statement of deception as a necessary part of evolutionary adaptation to rationalizing sin as a necessity in the hands of humans.

We rationalize our own acts as necessary means to an end. Getting a job by destroying someone else's reputation is rationalized as, "I know I gossiped about her, but I was more suited for the job than she was." Cheating on income tax is disguised as, "I lied to the IRS about my income, but I can put the money to much better use than they can." If our plumb line is the objective truth of God, these rationalizations and manipulations won't work. Sin is raw and real and ugly, and it must be called by name with no attempt at decontaminating its toxic sting.

Part one of a good confession is to examine our conscience and honestly identify our sin. Part two is being genuinely sorry for that sin.

Having a godly sorrow for our sins. What good is an egg whose shell cannot be broken? If you can't break through the shell, the goodness inside cannot be accessed. And an egg whose shell is too fragile is no good either. It must always be carefully kept until time for its use.

Our spirits are the same. A spirit that is never broken has no concept of the horror of its sin. And a spirit that is too frail and breaks at anything has no faith in the act of redemption.

Luke 13:5 says that unless we repent, we will perish. Repentance will not happen unless our spirits are broken at the thought of our sins. Casual regret or frustration at the resulting collateral damage of our sin is not what this brokenness is. It is also not regret at being caught. It is a recognition of our vileness in comparison to God's holiness. It is difficult to comprehend that our own failings are as lethal to Christ on the cross as other people's hideous acts. We can conjure up outrage at the dramatic sins of murder, child abuse, and cold disregard for life. But the unbearable joy of the story is that Christ died for all sin. He did not have to merely break his leg or stub his toe for our mild indiscretions, but he hung until his life breathed out of him. And this very personal understanding, that he would have done it just for me, should be enough to break my heart wide open and spill my spirit in undryable tears. As John R. W. Stott put it, "Tears like this are the holy water which God is said to store in his bottle"[5] (see Ps. 56:8).

Matthew's account of Christ speaking about godly character paradoxically reminds us that "happy are those who mourn" (Matt. 5:4). The Greek word used here for "mourn" means a deep lament with unrestrainable tears. The main message of this concise beatitude is that those who have deep sorrow for the tragedy of their sin are blessed and will be comforted. William

Barclay wrote, "The way to the joy of forgiveness is through the desperate sorrow of the broken heart."[6] If we are to receive the comfort of forgiveness, we will mourn our sin.

In 2 Corinthians 7:10, Paul eloquently expanded on the theme by making the distinction between godly sorrow and worldly sorrow. One brings life with no regrets and one brings death. True godly sorrow is not a conjured-up package of "chick-flick tears." It is not mere surface emotions that come from a thin skin, but deep private wailing.

Please be aware that there is a difference between conviction and condemnation, between good guilt and bad guilt. Conviction over our sins begins with the Holy Spirit revealing ourselves to us when we examine our conscience. This Holy Spirit-led journey then brings godly sorrow, which leads to repentance, the outward change in our actions that reflects the inward mourning. Condemnation, on the other hand, brings worldly sorrow, which leads to depression and an inability to function. It is worldly sorrow that sits and whines about life's woes and makes your attempts at living impotent. Worldly sorrow makes getting out of bed more trouble than it is worth, and it makes coping a distant memory. Throw off your clutter, dear friend, and hear the voice of Christ, who freed the woman caught in her scarlet-letter sin, saying, "I do not condemn you" (John 8:11). Pause and make the "you" personal. Hear Christ's simple absolution in your spirit.

Condemnation declares "unfit for use." Conviction pleads the blood of Christ. If you are living in a debilitating state of guilt, you are not under the conviction of the Holy Spirit. You are under a worldly sorrow that strips the life from you. God's loving conviction leads us to a sincere, gut-wrenching sorrow for our sin, but it also brings life and restoration.

When we have a godly sorrow over our sin, that conviction leads to *repentance,* a contrite spirit dedicated to amending behavior.

At crawling age, I was confident and definitely on the move. I had an affinity for things that dangled at my level. We had a potted plant in our house that crept and crawled its way out of the pot and over the edge of the table, hanging within my reach, begging me to pull it whenever I passed it. And I faithfully did. My philodendron fetish was not a popular new trick with my parents, but they had far more concern over my attraction to electric cables. Didn't they understand that I *needed* to pull the chords out of those horrible slits in the wall holding them captive? After several stern scoldings, in which my father explained to me that I shouldn't do that and why, he said, "Do you understand?" and I stared into his face and nodded my head yes. I then turned to the electric cable and yanked it out of the wall.

While repentance is more than the conditional obedience of early childhood, it is incomplete without a change in behavior. Understanding that something is wrong is the interior part of the lesson. Aligning one's behavior to reflect that understanding is the exterior part. One without the other is incomplete.

Thinking that we are able to change our behavior by sheer willpower is the first step toward failure. The "good girl" in us wants to believe that we can be good enough on our own if we try. We just can't. Paul spoke (Rom. 8:15) confessionally, saying that he couldn't change his own behavior by just determining to do so. He also reminds us that it is God's work within us that helps us have "the want to want to," and then helps us to do it (Phil. 2:13).

One Christmas, my mom had learned to make sourdough bread. The smell of the freshly baked loaf each morning paled only to the flavor. My sister and I were instant converts, and Mom gave us both some "starter" to take home with us. "Starter" is the fermented culture saved from one baking to use in the next. I have no idea how it is made because my mother gave it to me. She has no idea how it is made because her neighbor gave it to her, and so on. I took mine home and had the patience to keep up with it for about three weeks. My sister's blew up on the airplane trip home. While our commitment to the bread experience was short-lived, the "starter" Mom gave us was the symbol of our "want to want to" bake bread.

Exactly how much the process of repentance comes down to our personal responsibility and how much is the work of the Holy Spirit has been debated by theologians for decades. I do know the Spirit is mysterious. I don't know how it happens—sometimes in prayer, sometimes in reading the Scripture, sometimes in fasting, sometimes in taking a quiet walk, but I am given the "want to want to" change my behavior. And it is this "starter" that the Holy Spirit uses to produce results of changed behavior in my life (Heb. 13:20–21; Gal. 5:22–25).

What we are speaking of here is the pattern that we began with (Heb. 12:1): "Let us lay aside the sin that so easily entangles us." If we have no change in behavior, we will become more and more entangled, and the goal of simplifying our lives will be defeated.

Our beloved first dog Sienna was playing like a cat with the curtains hanging over our sliding glass door one day in her puppyhood. She pulled the end down from the curtain rod and somehow pierced her paw with the hook. In her struggle to free herself, she tangled herself more and more in the curtain until she became tethered to the window. When I came home and discovered her, my heart broke. I removed the rest of the curtain from the rod and gathered it up with her in my arms and frantically drove her to the vet. With no residual blood or impairment, the vet pulled the hook out, and Sienna jumped off the examining table and scampered down the hall. This bright dog never jumped up on the curtains again. I should learn so quickly.

FORGIVENESS

When your spirit is cluttered with sin, the act of Christ's forgiveness is what ultimately unclutters it. When we have grieved our sin and repented, He will lift us up (James 4:10), and as my husband Jim poetically put it, "grace will replace disgrace."

Do you feel that your shame is too much for Christ to forgive? Consider King David, who was called a "man after God's heart." This godly man gave in to bad choices resulting in heavy collateral damage. He looked out his window and saw Bathsheba bathing on her rooftop. He desired her, set his mind to have her, and sent her husband to his death to get her. And God not only forgave him but also included him in the lineage of Christ.

Consider the woman who had "many sins" (Luke 7:47) and was a well-known prostitute. She crashed a luncheon and unself-consciously washed Jesus' feet with her tears, dried them with her hair, kissed them, and poured expensive perfume on them. The Pharisee host, who had invited Jesus and not the woman, insulted Jesus for obviously not knowing what kind of woman she was. Jesus contrasted her contrite spirit with the self-proclaimed holy man, and her sins were forgiven.

Consider Peter, who had walked with Christ as one of the Twelve. Jesus told him that he would deny him three times before the cock crowed. When Jesus was arrested, as they walked him through the courtyard, Peter denied knowing him for the third time. The rooster crowed, and Peter turned to see Christ looking straight at him. Even with the intense personal shame he felt, he was forgiven and became the rock that the church was built on.

Consider the people who crucified Christ. "Father, forgive them . . ." (Luke 23:34).

Philip Yancey quotes Walter Wink, saying, "The contagion of holiness overcomes the contagion of uncleanness." It is scandalous, and impossible, that our wretchedness is trumped by Christ's forgiveness. The truth is that our forgivability is not the issue. The issue is *who* the Forgiver is. At my very best, I am not deserving. William Langland said, "And all the wickedness in the world that man might work or think is no more to the mercy of God than a live coal in the sea."

I am not trying to confess "worm-ness" here, or insult the dignity of myself as a work in progress. But there is honestly no good reason why the God of all doing and being, of all goodness and pure holiness, should care for or forgive someone who regularly dishonors the act of the cross with careless or intentional sin. But he does.

There is a story of a Spanish father and son who had become estranged. After months of searching for the runaway son, the father placed an add in the Madrid newspaper that read: "Dear Paco, meet me in front of this newspaper office at noon on Saturday. All is forgiven. I love you. Your father." To his surprise, Saturday at noon the father was greeted by eight hundred Pacos, looking for forgiveness and love from their fathers.[7]

The invitation for love and forgiveness from our heavenly Father is written in 1 John 1:9: "If we confess our sins, he is faithful and just to forgive us our sins, and to cleanse us from all unrighteousness" (KJV). It is not the free-for-all call in the childhood game of hide-and-seek. We misunderstand if we equate "free" with "grace." "Free" is no charge to anyone, but "grace" is charged to another's account. This invitation is a grace-filled promise of forgiveness, purchased by a Father with the blood of his Son.

SIMPLE SUMMARY

In 1910, Luther and Charlotte Gulick established the Camp Fire Girls, the first nonsectarian organization for girls in the United States. In 1966, I became a Camp Fire Girl. In keeping with my personality, I did not want to join the commonly accepted girls' group, and so while most of my peers were wearing green dresses and selling cookies, I wore navy blue and white and sold peanuts. At our first meeting, we selected names from combining significant Native American syllables. I proudly named myself "Wahota," meaning "smiling April sunshine."

The first event where we wore our uniforms, I was a victim of "bead-envy." You see, instead of earning merit patches that were sewn onto sashes, we Camp Fire Girls earned beads to sew onto our vests. The color and quantity of the beads showed our expertise in areas of service, cooking, leadership, and various other important areas that I have since forgotten. Some girls had so many beads sewn to their vests that you could barely see the fabric. I committed in my very young, overachieving heart that I would earn so many beads they would have to give me a floor-length vest to hold them all, and I vowed I would never show up to a CFG event beadless again. I slept in a tent and learned to cook pancakes on a coffee can. Cha-ching! I served my parents breakfast in bed. Cha-ching! I picked up trash on the school playground. Cha-ching! The sound of beads collecting in my jar. I wandered the neighborhood in my crisp white shirt, navy blue skirt, vest, and beanie, imploring friends and strangers to purchase multiple cans of peanuts. This earned me "high-sales award," which netted major beads. And before the next event, my mother sewed beads to my vest until she thought her fingers would bleed. I proudly and confidently walked in, sure that no one could possibly have as many beads as I, and before I reached the table assigned to me and the other CFGs from Taylor Elementary School, I discovered that I had been out-beaded by at least two other girls I had seen and, I suspected, by one other girl I couldn't bear to look at but whose beads made a clicking sound hitting one another as they hung like fringe below the bottom of her vest. I quit Camp Fire Girls a year later, exhausted in my never-ending pursuit of beads.

Even now, I try to earn beads with God by having a long quiet time, praying without sleeping (or was that "ceasing?"), and not sinning nearly as bad as other people do. But no matter how many beads I earn, nothing can earn me God's love. His unbelievable grace is not acquisitionable. My works-oriented logic was broken on the door frame of grace, and my sin and good works all spilled out before me as worthless. God will never love me more and never love me *less* than he does in this moment. This is revelational truth, particularly for those of us who tend toward being performance driven in our faith. Erwin Lutzer eloquently states: "Christ's death on the cross included a sacrifice for all our sins, past, present, and future. All of our sins were future when Christ died two thousand years ago. There is no sin that you will ever commit that has not already been included in Christ's death."

While we must not abuse God's pardon with careless living, there is nothing we can do to earn the forgiveness bought for us with every smack of the nail through his Son's hands. It is merely conditional on our recognizing that we are sinners in the hands of a holy God. And the confession that leads to a change in behavior—and results in unbelievable forgiveness—reduces the clutter in our spirit.

10

PERSEVERING IN THE EVERYDAY

There is a simplicity of pure intention that sees life as a divine appointment with daily devotion. The "Grand A-Ha" is not over once we have met the Savior. It is only beginning. A. W. Tozer wrote in *The Pursuit of God*, "To have found God and still to pursue Him is the soul's paradox of love."

It seems that the common evangelical term "becoming a Christian" has lost its true meaning. There is so much emphasis on the initial "salvific moment" that the lifetime of "becoming" gets less than back-page billing. Granted, our spiritual birth is truly a notable moment, but there is a lot more "becoming" than "birthing." After 20 years of marriage, Jim and I find that there is much more celebrating in the cumulative years of our commitment than in the memory of our wedding day. In the same way, the commitment we make to Christ is celebrated by our ongoing commitment to daily spiritual fidelity.

I grieve the fact that many of my friends have made a sanctuary out of what was only intended to be the porch of the temple.[1] They made a commitment to know Christ, but because of either a lack of discipling or discipline, or both, they haven't progressed past the point of the front porch and entered into the astonishing marvel of relationship with Christ. And they have become accustomed to the sparseness of their spiritual lives.

Can you imagine being content to stand in the entrance of the Louvre and never go inside to see the Da Vinci, El Greco, Rembrandt, or Van Eyck paintings? Or to stand outside the Vienna Opera house while José Carreras sang inside? Or to sit in the parking lot and not go through the gate of the Biltmore House Estate to view the gardens? Or to stand in the Kauai airport but never venture out to view the black sand beaches and postcard-perfect waterfalls? Or to meet Christ and then not pursue a relationship? Habits of Holiness that mark a disciple are a far more difficult sell than tickets to heaven are. Discipleship needs a better press agent.

Eugene Peterson's book *A Long Obedience in the Same Direction* is titled after the Friedrich Nietzsche quote: "The essential thing 'in heaven and earth' is . . . that there should be long obedience in the same direction; there thereby results, and has always resulted in the long run, something which has made life worth living." In his call to discipleship, Eugene Peterson reminds us that we are spiritual pilgrims, not tourists with a mere passing interest in spiritual things.

When I was very young, our family would make visits to Cape Cod to see my father's parents, frequently around Thanksgiving. The house on Ocean Street was walking distance from downtown and blended in with the quaint wooden houses of Hyannis. Grandmother was an intensely devout Christian woman, involved in all the programs of her local church, and, most important to me, she worked in the bakery on the corner. We would walk there every day so I could get a chocolate-chip and a toffee-chip cookie. They were as big and round as my heavily cheeked face.

Granddad was a multitalented man who faithfully worked a variety of jobs to pay the bills, but his love was in his after-work hours. A renaissance man, he painted oil-paintings, made silver jewelry, played piano and sang in Vaudeville, performed as a magician, and even met Houdini. I enjoyed hours watching him do the things he loved, and even discovered myself in some of his pursuits.

These childhood trips also nurtured in me my father's love of the ocean. He and I would walk down Ocean Street early in the morning and watch the local marina wake up. Sometimes we would drive out to Sandy Neck Beach where my granddad worked at the recreational center. Wrapped like a walking package in scarf, hat, mittens, and various other cold weather accoutrements, I would walk the beach. The cold November winds whipped my hair across my face and stung my cheeks. The Atlantic looked deep and unknowable from the horizon to the sand at my feet. It always amazed me how dark and unknowable it appeared until I held it in my hand. In that sense, I could know the ocean, one handful at a time.

That is the way of the Spirit. We will only know the wonder of a relationship with God one day at a time. If we are to pursue knowing God past our initial encounter and develop a relationship that will result in our taking on more of the image of Christ, I suggest five habits of holiness to keep us in his presence: (1) meditation, (2) prayer, (3) fasting, (4) the Eucharist, and (5) worship.

MEDITATION

The Mariana Trench is the deepest sea canyon, at 35,802 feet. That is a little higher than planes typically fly, and if Mt. Everest were dumped into the trench, there would still be about a mile of water above it. If a hurricane were ravaging the surface, all would be still and quiet in the trench. Still waters run deep, says the English proverb. Shakespeare's Henry VI phrases the same thought: "Smooth runs the water where the brook is deep."

If we are to escape the busyness ravaging our lives, we must brave the deep world of the interior.

When we were on a missions trip in Bluefield, West Virginia, on our day off we joined several junior highers on a rafting trip down the New River. Our guides had told us to watch for smooth water for easy passage. After splashing and nearly drowning our way down rough white water, rock-infested rapids in anything but smooth water, I was more than mildly relieved to reach a long stretch called "the pool." This was deep water as smooth as a frozen pond. It was also perfect for swimming, and most of the students abandoned the rafts. I noticed, while we paddled along, the perfect replica of the hillsides and clouds above reflected in the water. It is only in still water that a clear reflection can be seen.

Likewise, if we want the image of God to be clearly reflected in us, we must be still.

Still and deep. These are distinctives of the contemplative life of the Spirit. Meditation places us ever in the presence of the infinite and reminds us of our creatureliness. It is the essential in preparing us for persevering in the Spirit. All contemplative habits of holiness are intensified when we take the time to quiet ourselves. George A. Buttrick said: "We should not rush into the Presence; the church of private devotion should be entered through the vestibule in an orderly quietness." Meditation is the vestibule.

This time is essential preparation. While eastern thought on meditation is that of emptying oneself, Christian meditation is about quieting the interior so as to then be able to fill it with the presence of God. Charles Swindoll says that meditation is a lost art in our century. He defines meditation as "disciplined thought, focused on a single object or Scripture for a period of time." In the "hurry, be productive" nature of our culture, time of still quietness has become untreasured. The pressure to accomplish and achieve leaves us too stressed to even consider the habit of meditation. But if we truly desire to simplify our lives and clearly reflect the image of Christ, we will trade in our "white-water living" for still, deep water. So, he says to us, "Be still, and know that I am God" (Ps. 46:10, KJV). In the silencing awe of the moment, we run out of words and sit in the mystery.

Sitting in the mystery will take practice and patience. Morton Kelsey reminds us that in nature, growth cannot be forced. However, given just the right environment and plenty of time, the sequoia sempervirens of northern California and southern Oregon will sprout from a tiny seed, a pound of which would contain more than one hundred thousand, and grow as tall as 350 feet and live as long as two thousand years. Patience and the appropriate environment produce the mighty redwood. We must know enough not to disturb a tiny seedling as it sprouts but give it time to grow roots and develop. For the seed of meditation to grow in our spirits, we will need to plant a viable seed of time, nurture it with the right environment, and not rush the results.

Don't expect to go from unloading the groceries to the contemplative ecstasies of Teresa of Avila, who was so overcome with spiritual joy that she said her "face was shining and rosy, and her eyes shone like candles."[2] Before you snarl, know that even she had times of spiritual torment. But her devotion to spiritual life was a lifelong journey. We somehow have to push away the distractions of our selves to the "cloud of forgetting" and aim for heaven. As we commune with God, the Spirit works within us to make us more Christlike (2 Cor. 3:18). Augustine taught, "The more the soul extends itself to that which is eternal, the more it is reformed according to the image of God."

When you commit to a time of stillness, you will discover that your language center requires activity. The first few minutes of quiet are fine, but then you will begin to run a movie on the inside of your eyelids. It is helpful to give your mind something to dwell on. You could focus on an attribute of God like "provider," "peace," "mighty counselor," or, as Charles Swindoll suggested, you could focus on a particular Scripture verse, or a particular promise or truth that God is realizing in you. Some have suggested focusing on the word *maranatha,* which means "Come, Lord Jesus." I find that as I attempt to slow down and shut my eyes, as I deliberately breathe in and out, I will begin to calm down and know the presence of the Spirit. It is not a magical incantation, but a pure and simple prayer. It is also not the insincere lip labor or vain repetitions spoken of in Matthew 6:7, but utterings of a heart longing to be in the presence of God. Thomas Merton said it is an "orientation of our whole body, mind, and spirit to God in silence, attention, and adoration."[3]

If you find your mind continuing to wander, don't throw up your hands in disgust and quit. Gently bring your attention back to a simple focus on the Lord, and he will honor it and begin to perfect his strength in your weakness.

When I was five, I planted a popsicle stick just outside of our apartment door in the dirt of a roughly designated flower bed, in the dark corner behind a large juniper. I don't know if it was an active imagination or pure stubborn ignorance, but I was convinced it would grow into a Popsicle tree. I imagined the joyous treat it would be to harvest those Popsicles once the tree grew. Long after the red dye from that cherry Popsicle had faded from my tongue and lips, there was still no sign of any tree. Unlike the redwood tree, which can grow even a foot or two each year, my Popsicle tree did not come from a viable seed, nor was it planted in a nurturing environment. And no matter how much I believed it would grow, I could not "want" it into being.

A faithful commitment to meditation, a quiet time in the "vestibule," will lead naturally into a time of sincere prayer.

PRAYER

I have finally changed into my pajamas, removed my makeup, washed my face, applied my eye cream, night cream and lip moisturizer, brushed and flossed my teeth, gargled with mouthwash, and removed all jewelry. I approach the bed, where I growl a low expression of envy at my husband who has already been in bed for twenty minutes, not having nearly as many regimens to complete before he can sleep. Being in this perfectly anything-but-contemplative state, I fall down and pull the comforter up around me, put my *I Love Lucy* night blinders on and stuff my ear plugs into my ears and begin "Now I lay me down to sleep . . ." and give up in frustration, deciding I'll pray in the morning.

Morning comes despite my attempts to fool my body with the night blinders, and I give it a "Good morning, Lord. Be with me and everyone today. More later. Over and out." And I hit the ground running with plans to complete all the things I didn't complete yesterday, as well as a few extras.

That night, as I am removing my makeup and washing my face, I am convicted that I haven't spent more time in prayer that day and commit that when I lie down I will enjoy the quiet darkness with the Lord and cover the bases with him. And once again, I am in the deep drool of sleep before I have even really begun to pray.

If you have felt even a remotely similar frustration with your prayer life, you are normal. I have begun to discover that contemplative habits of holiness suffer from the pressures of busyness in our culture and are easily abandoned when we consider simplifying our lives. But communication with God is far more relevant and necessary than any busyness we can contrive. It's just that the nature of prayer, as with meditation, demands the quiet that is so much a premium in our schedules. And the abstract qualities of having a conversation with an unseeable heavenly Father add the extra dimension of unfamiliarity in western culture. And so I beg the Lord to compel me to come spend time in his presence, and trust that if I linger, he will meet me.

It is important to be freed from the pressure that prayer must be some complex form of communication requiring seminarian vocabulary. I remember the story of the young boy who went to a prayer meeting with his grandmother. She sat him in the last pew with books and coloring activities, and said to be quiet while she joined the group up front for prayer. After hearing prayers of formal "thee's" and "thou's" prayed in perfect King James language, the boy stood up on the pew and yelled "Dear God, a, b, c, d, e . . ." and prayed the entire alphabet, closing in a confident "Amen!" He explained to his grandmother that since he didn't know all the words, he gave all the letters to God and let him make them into the words. The simplicity of prayer is the pure honesty of our childlike hearts poured out to our heavenly Father. Bring your tired, your defeated, your frustrated and lonely self to the Father, who waits with open arms.

It is not just eloquent words spoken in lovely relationship to each other, but neither is it a "to-do" list we deliver to God. This isn't prayer, it is genie lamp rubbing. While "gimmee" prayers, shopping lists, "I'm in a jam" prayers, "bargaining" prayers (God, if you . . . , then I . . .), and last-ditch prayers are graciously listened to by our loving and patient Father, they are not signs of mature and loving disciples. This is not to discourage early efforts at prayer, but it is to encourage us as spiritual pilgrims to move beyond the shallow nature of "me-oriented" conversation with God and pursue the depth and unplumbed fathoms of intimacy with the infinite.

So just what exactly is prayer? Even the disciples, who had prayed all their lives, asked Jesus to teach them how to pray. He gave us the Lord's Prayer and the many occasions of his own praying as examples to follow. From these we see that we must pray our doubt, our faith, our concerns, our fears, our future, our dreams, our thanks, our sins, and our intercessory concerns. Most importantly, as Henri Nouwen said, prayer must be an interior, unceasing doxology. It must include constant praise and recognition of him to whom we pray. It is dialogue, and it is quiet listening. A secret combination of words will not unlock the mysteries of the Spirit, but an honest outpouring will bring the mysterious peace of God that passes all understanding (Phil. 4:6–7).

The ultimate goal of praying without ceasing, which is being constantly mindful of the presence of God—and "flash prayers," as Frank Laubach has suggested, when to see or hear someone is to pray for them—is what maturity in our prayer life will produce. But even then, we will need to continue to have specific times of prayer. We need to have a plan of *when* and *where*, and an idea of *how* won't hurt. As George A. Buttrick said, prayer "is not formal, but it is not formless; it has its cultivation, its behavior . . . its disciplines."

You will find seasons when one approach will be more successful for you than others. Adjusting for this will help keep your prayer life fresh. And while you need to be flexible, a commitment to a time and place is good when you begin this habit. It might be in a stall in the ladies' room on your afternoon break at work. It may be in your favorite chair after everyone else leaves the house in the morning.

We plan to build a house in the next few years and I've already designed a space for my spiritual "place" that will have a small chair to sit in, and my very old and humble prayer bench. I plan to deck it out with candles and favorite devotional books, as well as a wall of reminders where I can post Scripture I want or need to meditate on. The important thing is to have a place and time that you can identify and commit to. We have places where we bathe, sleep, eat, and work out, so why not a place where we spend time with the Lord? Giving your commitment some form will make it harder to skip.

I love to read prayers. It helps to express the unverbalized thoughts of my spirit and warms up my mind to speak my own thoughts. John Baillie's *A Diary of Private Prayer* is a collection of his very vulnerable and comprehensive prayers. "Here am I, O God, of little power and of mean estate . . . Thou art hidden behind the curtain of sense, incomprehensible in Thy greatness, mysterious in Thine almighty power; yet here I speak with Thee familiarly as child to parent, as friend to friend." In dry or numb times, the words of another pilgrim can help take you before the Father. *Little Book of Prayers,* which is a collection by contributors like François Fenelon, Augustine, and Thomas à Kempis, Lancelot Andrews' *Private Devotions,* and Eugene Peterson's *Praying with the Psalms,* are also excellent sources.

Some form of a prayer journal can also be helpful. Writing out praises of who God is, as well as personal thoughts and concerns, can help you to concentrate and stay focused. It also can help remind you of his faithfulness when you read back over it later. Writing in an empty book of paper, making notes on a daily calendar, or using a grease board and pen are all practical ways of noting prayers.

Having a prayer partner can be encouraging as well as build accountability in your prayer life. You can even do this by e-mail, regular mail, or telephone. An extended family prayer list that is circulated and added to will help you be aware of each other's needs and remind you to pray for them. But if you do spend time praying with someone else, don't eliminate your own personal time with God. Nothing can replace going to the Father vulnerable and honest, and that will only happen when you are alone with him.

Make your goals realistic in the beginning, or you will defeat yourself quickly. Even the hard-working robin in my backyard understood that she must build her nest over the back door one twig at a time. So she started soon enough that it was finished when she needed it. Likewise, pray for a short time each day, or each week, and you will be able to build it up more and more. Your endurance and vocabulary will grow, as will your desire to pray. And it will become easier for you to recognize the sound of God's voice, prompting you in your spirit, because you have spent time with him. And as you linger, he will meet you.

FASTING

It is the first time I am hosting a family gathering and I am remarkably relaxed. The dressing, fruit salad, and apple pies are made and the sweet potato casserole is ready to be picked up. My mom and dad and Jim and I have gone to the local grocery store whose cranberry and turkey supplies are spent, to pick up last-minute items like coffee that Jim and I are unaccustomed to having in our supply. My sister and her husband and their now grown-up (which I am in denial about) daughter will arrive Thanksgiving morning. By 4 o'clock that afternoon, I pray, with all fingers crossed, we will sit to share in a meal of abundance and thankfulness.

While we shop, my father, who is as fanatical as I am about Christmas and all that goes with it, is attentive to my longing glances at the early signs of seasonal commerce. The poinsettias are in. Large and small plants wrapped in gold, red, or green foil line the display shelves of the fresh flower department, strategically placed near the front door. There are cream ones and pink ones, but I would never think of straying from the traditional red. And as if we have communicated telepathically, before we get to the check-out counter, Dad has selected the two prime specimens and placed them in the upper part of his basket. I am already planning where I will put them so that we can enjoy them during our meal the next day. And before the Christmas season was over, I would have purchased nine more poinsettias, doomed to dry out and be thrown in the garbage sometime in January.

Joel Roberts Poinsett, United States ambassador to Mexico from 1825 to 1829, fell in love with these festive plants and brought cuttings back to his plantation in Greenville, South Carolina. A British-educated botanist, he propagated and distributed them and eventually gave them his name. And I am grateful to Mr. Poinsett for his pioneering efforts in the field of Christmas decorations.

The plants never survive more than a season in my house, but my mother faithfully brought hers to flower year after year. Sorry little excuses for botany would line the Ping Pong table in her basement. They would be in total darkness throughout the night, and she would faithfully go down and turn on the fluorescent light that hung directly above them each morning. And by Christmas, the transformation was unbelievable. I think where I went wrong in this horticultural assignment was that I heard the part about "put them in the basement," but not the part about "give them light and water." The whole thing is a delicate process, and not one that makes a lot of sense to me.

Poinsettias are short-day plants. When the daylight is only twelve hours or less, starting around Thanksgiving, they begin to show color in their bracts, the modified leaves we consider to be the flower. But before this annual show of Christmas color, they must be in total darkness from 5 P.M. to 8 A.M., every night, October through Thanksgiving. Any light exposure between those hours will threaten the flowering. The denial of light causes the plant to reduce its production of chlorophyl and unmasks the red that was hiding beneath the green. I would never have imagined that withholding one of the few necessities of life from a plant would cause it to blossom.

Likewise, fasting, denying the flesh one of its most natural necessities—

food—causes the inner life to blossom (2 Cor. 4:16)[4]. It can enhance our prayer life, affirm a clearer and intensified connection with God, result in guidance and grace for specific decisions and trials, and produce a general feeling of spiritual renewal. And while the many benefits are desirable, we must maintain our first intention to be God inspired and God directed.

Fasting lost its place in our experience because, at one point, many thought of it as too penitential. It had the ring of "earning" our redemption. But as is the case in many overreactions, the eliminating of it entirely was an extreme that cost us an essential part of persevering in the Spirit, of being in the Presence. There are many references to fasting in Scripture. While never delivered in the context of a "thou shalt," the suggestion to fast is more than implied. It was certainly a part of Jewish life in the Old Testament,[5] and Christ refers to it with "*when* you fast" (Matt. 6:16), as well as by the example of his forty-day fast in preparation of ministry (Matt. 4)[6] in the New Testament. It was an assumed part of the Christian experience and almost always linked with prayer. Clearly, if we desire the benefits of purification, self-control, and spiritual renewal, we will fast.

The physical benefits of cleansing and purifying we derive from fasting are also afforded our spirits. In the denial of food, we are unmasked to discover the things that control us so that we can then surrender and be transformed more into the image of Christ. Richard Foster says that when things like anger or bitterness are in us, they will surface when we fast. At first, we will want to blame those things on our hunger, but the Holy Spirit will give us the realization that they were masked within us to begin with. At that point, as we surrender, our spirits are being purified, much as our physical bodies are being purified. And like the poinsettia, we bloom as we are unmasked.

When we say "no" to our appetite, we see how little food we truly need to be sustained. And with each impulse to eat, often instigated more by habit than actual hunger, as we say "no," we are building self-control in our spirits. As we strengthen our resolve by saying "no" here, we discover that we can say "no" to other appetites. Self-control breeds self-control. You will find that as you build confidence in fasting, the Holy Spirit will give you confidence to battle other temptations and addictions. I remember when I was struggling with a habit of turning on the television in the afternoons. If I said "yes" and turned it on, it remained on all afternoon. There is nothing inherently wrong with this, except that I felt out of control. My experience with fasting built my confidence to say "no" to that appetite, and, day by day, I felt released as I said "no" to the magnet of television distraction. The poet Ranier Maria Rilke spoke of the misuse and squandering of physical pleasure. He said that it is the attempt to apply it "as a stimulant at the tired spots of our lives"[7] that dulls our understanding of our true needs. Saying "no" to the physical to say "yes" to the spiritual becomes an empowering experience.

Spiritual renewal is by far the most valued result of fasting. The unique state of body and mind that fasting places us in makes it easier to tune in to the interior connection of the Spirit. Fasting and prayer often result in revelation, peace, confirmation, strength, and resolve. For us flesh-and-blood dwellers, who struggle with the mysterious, amorphous realm of the Spirit, fasting gives us tangible means of making the connection. The clearness of mind and lucidity that come with fasting help alert our spirit for those impressions of direction and leading that God might communicate to us. It is not always a "writing on the wall" experience, but it is always an affirming sense of God's presence.

While there are times when corporate fasting is appropriate, I am focusing on the personal fast here. It is helpful to do with someone, especially your mate or those you share a home with. Most recently, Jim and I agreed to fast during daylight hours for Lent. Having each other to be accountable to and to encourage made the experience better.

There are many types of fasts that last a variety of times. You can fast lunch every day or fast all day once a week. The options are endless, but the important thing is the experience. We chose to do a juice fast for the forty days of Lent. We started by fasting every other day and found that to have less impact than we desired. So we committed to every day, bought a juicer, and enjoyed the treat of fresh fruit juice once a day. The first week, I found the hours of 3 to 5 P.M. so difficult. At the suggestion of a friend, I chose those times to pray and ask the Lord to fill my emptiness. By the second week, those were truly some wonderful times of communing with God. I will admit that we found our noses glued to the window, awaiting sundown on several days, but we both came out of the experience feeling cleansed physically and spiritually, as well as having sensed the inner world of the Spirit more intimately. We also came to appreciate the freedom of eating at will more than we ever had before.

Any long fast, particularly with water only, should be done with medical supervision. But if you are healthy and able, some form of fasting is a habit of holiness that will become an essential once you have done it. Fasting gives opportunity for the Spirit of the living God to fall afresh on us. And as we sit in the presence of the God of our affection, our spiritual life will bloom.

THE EUCHARIST

At six years old, as I began my Sunday church service ritual of filling in the "o's" in the bulletin, I read the order of service and discovered it was the Lord's Supper Sunday. For me, that meant longer to sit on those pews designed by comfort-scorning ascetics. After the pastor finished the sermon—and I always thought it was inconsiderate of him not to shorten it on Lord's Supper Sunday—eight men would march to the front of the church, several buttoning the middle button of their dark suit coats as they walked. Stacks of round silver plates and communion cup holders would be distributed to them, and they would silently pass out the elements of "body" and "blood." I resented the trays being passed right over me; I may not have been old enough to partake, but I was certainly capable of passing the trays on my own. Sometimes I was allowed to hold the cracker for my mom or dad, and I would lick my fingertips to try and distinguish the flavor. It was strange to me; there was no salt flavor. After they ate the cracker and drank the juice, my parents would let me put the small cups into the holders mounted on the back of the pew in front of us. During prayer, with every head bowed and every eye closed, I would put the cup to my mouth and run my tongue around the inside of it, devouring any trace of grape juice that lingered. An older grandmotherly woman who had hard candy in her purse carefully unwrapped the noisy clear paper and gave the candy to me with a smile. But even as the sweet sugar dissolved on my tongue, I longed for the day when I would be old enough to eat the stale, unsalted cracker and drink the tiny watered-down juice.

I love to attend the Episcopal church in Green Hills during Lent. The liturgy is so beautiful and the service so reverent. I also love it because they serve communion every Sunday. But it's funny how all these years later I still find myself in ascetic-designed pews wishing the homily would be over so we could finally get to communion. The Episcopal tradition shares the elements differently than the Southern Baptist church of my childhood. There are no men in dark suits passing out crackers and juice. Instead, the priest and laypeople (even women), dressed in long white robes, invite us to come to the altar and kneel to receive the wafer and to drink from the communal wine. They also offer communion by intinction. This is when the Eucharistic bread is dipped into the consecrated wine, and those of us who are hyper-paranoid about germs do not have to place our lips where a stranger has placed theirs. As I stood waiting anxiously for my turn, I watched our friends and their two daughters go forward to receive communion. While their parents went to the side of the altar that offered the communal cup, Kate and younger sister Maddy confidently marched to the intinction side, knelt, and cupped their tiny hands inside of each other and held them out in front of their faces. As they walked back to their pews, you could see their little tongues working to unstick the wafer from the roof of their mouths.

As I watched them, I remembered the first time I had ever seen the paper-like round wafer with the impression of the cross raised on its surface. It was July 20, 1969, at noon in a park in Fairfax, Virginia. I had gone to the church picnic with my Catholic friends who lived across the street. I bowled in their bowling league, played softball in their softball league, and now this young Baptist girl ate their strange communion wafer. I was amazed, later that night, that even though one of the greatest human achievements had taken place that day, the Apollo II commander Neil Armstrong had walked on the moon, it was the transparent wine-glazed wafer on my tongue that I couldn't stop thinking about.

Last year, when our band went to play at a Methodist youth event in the mountains of Estes Park, Colorado, the eight hundred junior and senior high students closed out the weekend event by sharing communion. Black-, white-, brown-, and olive-skinned students dressed in T-shirts with their weekend theme "Imagine Planet Jesus" brightly printed on them, distributed the elements of grapes and fish-shaped crackers to the anticipating crowd. The bishop, dressed in overalls and wearing a collection of bright friendship bracelets tied around her wrist, said, "God is great! Let's eat!"

The following week, we played at a camp in Front Royal, Virginia, for another gathering of Methodist students. Sunday morning, the group of 135 broke into smaller groups of about ten or twelve people. One person from each group went to the front of the room and collected a small baguette and cluster of grapes. In the unusually quiet room, students tore off a small piece of bread and a grape and were encouraged to feed someone in the group and deliver it with the message, "The body and blood of Christ, for you."

I've probably received communion in every conceivable form. While some forms have been more meaningful to me than others, my experience has shown me that it is not the form but what is remembered in the act that is important. In fact, the Scripture only gives one clear directive: "Do this in remembrance of me" (1 Cor. 11:23–26). The term *Lord's Supper* is only found once in the Bible (1 Cor. 11:20) and, while the implication of each is there, neither *Communion* nor *Eucharist* is used at all. Each term is appropriate, but Eucharist most expresses the experience for me. The word itself means both gratitude and favor. When we take the elements, we are remembering God's good favor and expressing our thanks. It communicates how the death of Christ made the communion between a holy God and sinful humanity possible.

Christ's choice of bread and wine for the symbols in this sacrament are particularly poignant as we consider persevering in the everyday. He did not select a fancy gourmet dessert and one-of-a-kind vintage, but he took the everyday elements of bread and table wine. It reminds me again that the provisional sacrifice of Christ's death, which purchased pardon for our sins, continues to invade the everyday nature of our lives. He is not only with us at church or retreats or spiritual events, but he is with us in our everyday lives.

Not only were the elements ordinary, but the act of eating was an everyday experience. Christ did not engage in some elaborate and complicated dance and say, "Do this in remembrance of me." He did not come to invade only our special occasions, but our everyday lives. As our physical bodies need nourishment daily, so do our spirits. By our mouths we feed our bodies; by faith our spirits receive nourishment. Because "faith comes by hearing, and hearing by the Word of God" (Rom. 10:17, NKJV), when we feed on the

Word, we nourish our spirits. As we participate in the Eucharist, we eat the bread, which is symbolic of Christ, "the Word made flesh" (John 1:14). The beautiful and poetic symbols remind us of our need to read the Word daily.

I want to be aware of Christ in my daily life as much as I wanted to take communion for the first time. And I want the time I spend in his presence to conform me more to his image. When I quietly prepare to receive a broken cracker, round wafer, fish cracker, or piece of bread, I remind myself of Christ's sacrifice of body and blood for me, and before the juice or wine dries from my tongue, I remember that he goes with me into my everyday life. And the sacrament of remembering becomes an encounter that continues.

WORSHIP

I had majored in art in college, but had never given myself time to explore painting as a form of expression. I had, however, painted a little when I was a child, under the tutelage of my artistic grandfather. In the basement of his Cape Cod home, I developed a deep affection for dirty paintbrushes, half-used tubes of paint, and freshly gessoed canvas. The wooden box with handle and latch that he had handmade to hold the tools of his craft was a virtual treasure chest for me. I loved the smells and the mysterious sticks with cloth wrapped around the ends and the palette knives and rags that were inside the box.

A few years ago, I fondly looked on as a dear friend invested herself in her painting. I admired her brushes and tubes and was transported to the basement in Hyannis. I could palpably feel the desire to paint well up in me. I bought some inexpensive supplies and tentatively applied myself. With minimal confidence and abundant joy, I churned out five or six canvases in the next few months.

We were celebrating Christmas in Orlando with my family that year. Most of the gifts had been opened and cooed over, but a small package under the tree had my name on it. Dad, who plays Santa every year, delivered it to me, and I mindlessly shredded the wrapping. A collection of five extremely high-quality professional brushes were humbly held together by a rubber band and wrapped crudely with no box or grand presentation. My eyes began to leak. Silenced, I turned to my husband and sank into the eyes of the one human being on this earth who could know me so well. The second gift I received was seeing my husband delight so in my delight. He knew me well enough to honor my talent with his gift, and he did it not because I needed the paintbrushes, but because he knew it would give me joy. And since his pursuit of his own joy in pleasing me was anything but selfish, he honored me by his delight in me.

What is worship? The Scottish catechism says that man's chief end is "to glorify God and enjoy Him forever." C. S. Lewis said, "In commanding us to glorify Him, God is inviting us to enjoy Him." Worship is to delight in God, as that is what he desires from us. Knowing him and loving him, not out of duty or obligation, but because it gives us joy, is worship. If we delight ourselves most in God (Ps. 37:4), we demonstrate that he is our most precious treasure. John Piper rephrases the catechism to say, "God is most glorified in us when we are most satisfied in Him."[8]

I have a friend who says worship is not a shallow invitation to "cheeriness" but an invitation to "taste and see that the LORD is good" (Ps. 34:8, KJV). And when we taste of the abundant life of Christ, we will delight in the generosity of the goodness of God.

We must again possess that sense of wonder and awe about life and its mysteries if we are to worship with our whole hearts. Madeleine L'Engle, who is one of my most favorite wonder-muses, reminds us of Abraham Joshua Heschel mourning our "indifference to the sublime wonder of living." Each breath and heartbeat should be enough motivation for our worship, but if that weren't enough, to get our attention the Creator gave us a universe of stars, an ocean that faithfully returns to the sand in wave after wave, an entire genetic code in a drop of blood, and wonder upon wonder just waiting for our discovery. Augustine, in his classic work *The Confessions,* leads us to worship with his words: "Late have I loved you, O Beauty so ancient and so new; you breathed your fragrance upon me, and I drew in my breath and now I pant for you; I tasted you, and now I hunger and thirst for you."

Jim's expression of love toward me helps me put skin on the concept of worship. And while the intimacy we share with each other is a beautiful and godly gift, it can only foreshadow the feelings each of us has when struck with the undoing love and mercy of God. We must respond with worship by delighting in God and his wonders. And no lesser response would be due from a rescued heart to a Savior.

God's divine initiative of sending Christ as our substitute on the cross provokes our hearts to worship. When we contemplate the inequity of the arrangement, it must produce a humility that results in shouts of praise. The fact that we can trade in our tattered and wasted lives for a redeemed model, complete with the extras of unlimited love and forgiveness, is unparalleled. When I consider how excited I get about a good deal on deep-pocket, queen-sized sheets in 280-thread count, silky, 100-percent-cotton percale, my level of joy and expression of worship over my adoption into the kingdom are lame.

I suggest verbal expressions of praise and thanksgiving. Music, whether it is the elegant moodiness of classical or the joyous sounds of praise songs accompanied by all things loud, can bring my spirit to the doorway of worship. I also suggest walks of exploration among the wonders of this planet. It may not be in the grasses of the Serengetti, but the box turtles and moths in my backyard are equally intriguing. Attending corporate worship services, praying, reading Scripture, habits of holiness—all can escort you into the throne room where it would not be the least bit inappropriate to enter into a throne dance.

Exploding from heaven in the form of providential visitations is the acknowledged One. Ever making and shaping. Transcendent, recognized, and skinless. Limitless and beautiful. My brain swirls as holiness fizzes up through port. The earth's relentless turning is a flimsy attempt at time passing in comparison with the steady fire that burns in perpetual foreverness. Carry the weary to the gate. Lean one finger toward his exquisite honor. Pull away and be upside down in awkward awe.

Oh Father, hallowed be Thy name.

SIMPLE SUMMARY

We made a trip to Vienna, Austria, one mid-December. We had stopped in London to transition to European life, and then made our way to German-speaking Austria. It was our first time to visit somewhere we couldn't even read the signs for the "Ladies'" or "Men's" room. That was easily solved as "Toilet."

In anticipation of perfect apple strudel and gaudy Rococo architecture, we arrived in the center of downtown Vienna. Our quaint pension was three blocks from Stephansdom, or St. Stephen's Cathedral—the principal symbol of Vienna. It is in the center of the city, and its spire is 390 feet of Gothic expression. It is visible from anywhere in the city, and our explorations to see the art of Gustav Klimt, or the handmade ornaments in the outdoor Christmas-marts, or the Vienna Boys' Choir at the Hofburgkapelle, or sampling the local Bohemian fare at Café Hawelka, were always done in eyesight of the Stephansdom spire. Even though we couldn't speak the language, as long as we maintained that visual reference, we could find our way home.

In much the same way, habits of holiness keep us within spiritual eyesight of the God of heaven. As long as we maintain this reference, we can always find our way home as persevering pilgrims. While we enjoyed nearness-by-proximity with Stephansdom, habits of holiness help us stay close to God in what C. S. Lewis refers to as a "nearness-by-likeness." As he said, we had nothing to do with our being created in the image of God, but our imitation of God in this life is a *willed* imitation of God incarnate, Jesus.

Simplifying our spiritual lives requires a commitment to establishing healthy spiritual habits that place us in the middle of the joy of our salvation. And as failed and frail as our attempts are, by grace we must move into the nearness of God.

The image of God is in us. In the power of the Holy Spirit, we can nurture that image. If we plant Popsicle sticks, or imitation spirituality, we will not grow. In the words of Meister Eckhart: "The seed of God is in us. Given an intelligent and hard-working farmer, it will thrive and grow up to God. . . its fruits will be God-nature. Pear seeds grow into pear trees, nut seeds into nut trees, and God-seed into God." May God, through the power of the Holy Spirit, conform us more to his image as we persevere in the everyday.

11

FOCUSING ON
THE GOAL

Living on the small naval base in Yokosuka, Japan, at thirteen years old was one of the best things that ever happened to me. A new and intriguing culture to explore and the freedom that life on a U.S. military base provided gave me a safe place to test my wings. My dad was stationed on a cruiser that cruised its way to the waters off of Vietnam for 80 percent of the time, but the other 20 percent it was docked there on the base, and Dad slept in our house.

Junior high was such a time of discovery for me. I bought my first guitar, wrote my first song, had my first boyfriend, and endured the extreme hormonal swings of a preteen woman. I must emphasize preteen. I was four feet, six inches tall and weighed seventy-eight pounds with my hair, which flirted with my waist, dripping wet. And it was wet most of the time. I was a member of the swim team that practiced every day but Sunday at the Seafarer pool on the base. A young sailor was the coach, and it was clear that he probably had had issues with authority in his life. He blew the whistle, strutted, shouted instructions (really they were commands), and drove us like new recruits at boot camp. When my mother came to get me early one time and saw my tiny frame in the middle of the Olympic-sized pool, sputtering and spitting along, I thought she might pound the coach when he yelled at me to "get my gills moving." When she ran over to me with a towel as I effortlessly pulled my seventy-eight pounds from the ten-foot water, I was humiliated and reduced. My hair tucked into the tight swim team-style cap, my purple Speedo with the shoestring tied around the straps to keep them from falling off, and my chipmunk cheeks did not lend the intimidating image I hoped for as I rolled my eyes and muttered "Mom!" through lips puffy from the new braces beneath.

Tough as he was, that coach taught me a lot about discipline, will, toughing it out, and focus. My best stroke was the breaststroke, and my light little body popped out of the water just high enough to grab air and bobbed back down as quickly as anyone on the team. But in practice, everyone had to swim all the strokes. And even though the butterfly required the most sophistication and strength, it was the backstroke that continued to mess me up. I zigzagged across the pool like a bad EKG reading and ended up hitting my head on the side in total frustration. My feisty little spirit would not allow failure, and I would stroke harder to try to catch up, only to end up at the side again. Finally, my coach reached down and grabbed one of my hands and pulled me straight up out of the water. He marched me down to the shallow water, where we both jumped in.

Obviously not used to nurturing the shaky confidence of thirteen-year-old girls, he suggested that I didn't have a clue what I was doing. I rubbed my red-from-chlorine eyes and thanked him for his insight as he pushed my feet out from under me to get me on my back. One hand placed behind my waist to keep me afloat, he directed me to pick one of the telephone poles from the street and use it as my mark, then removed his hand and was out of the water and rearranging another young teen's self-esteem before I even sank beneath the surface.

I was not discouraged. Only challenged. I singled out one of the poles, began my stroke, and found myself at the other end of the pool, never having grazed the side once. That goal accomplished, I quit swim team and joined the bowling league.

In life just as in swimming no matter how hard you stroke, you won't get to the other side if you don't have your eyes fixed on a reference point.

We have come to the crucial part of this book. The information up to this point will help you simplify your life, enhancing the really important parts and, I hope, making the quality of life better. But now we come to the part that facilitates the whole. Jean Paul Sartre said a "finite point has no meaning without an infinite reference point." If our lives are to be focused and have meaning, we must "fix our eyes on the Author and perfecter of our faith" (Heb. 12:2). If we don't want to be bumping into things, zigzagging through mortality, we have to focus our spiritual eyes on God, our infinite reference point. He will give our lives direction and simplify the path of the journey.

François Fenélon suggested that we must "make brave resolutions to be wholly His." Making our minds up to be consumed by the presence of the living God is the ultimate step in simplifying our lives. When we dwell where his will is, the distractions and foolishness of life, all the vain things that charm us most, are laid down that we could embrace the Savior. And as we choose to live from the inside out, the Spirit who dwells within us will (1) build a hunger and thirst for righteousness, (2) drive us to develop a pure heart, and (3) give us faith to fix our gaze.

HUNGER AND THIRST

How much do we want to love God?[1] As long as he gives us comfort and joy, we will love him. But will we love him simply because he is the God of our hearts? When Christ spoke his message from the mountain (Matthew 5), he gave a list of characteristics that are marks of serious pilgrims. Christ said that if we would hunger and thirst for righteousness, we would be undeniably happy and satisfied. The Greek terms for *hunger* and *thirst* here are distinctly different from the typical use of the two verbs. It is not just a hunger for some bread, but the whole loaf. And not just a thirst for some water, but for the entire pitcher. Blessedness is not granted here for *doing* anything, but it is given in response to an extreme and intense longing and desire for the goodness of God. C. S. Lewis said it is not that God finds our desires too strong, but too weak. Too often we are in "like" with the notion of goodness and are content with the pale street lamp on our street, instead of having a desperate passion for righteousness that longs for all the lights of heaven.

If we are to have this insatiable hunger and thirst, we must logically be empty first. When I make the dreaded grocery run for our house, I usually wait until our cupboards are down to a can of smoked oysters and some chocolate pieces for making cookies, and until I am desperately starving. If I don't eat something before I get in the store, I'll buy two of anything and everything. That is the kind of hunger and thirst we need to have for righteousness. We have to empty ourselves of self, so that we can hunger and thirst, and then be filled with the goodness of God.

Theologians say that righteousness in this beatitude is not solely right relationship with God, but that it is simultaneously social justice. One is satisfied by the gift of salvation, and nothing can be done to earn it. The other will be satisfied in the kingdom of heaven, and works toward it through personal behavior and character in the community on earth. One is more about being, the other about doing.

I can't do anything to make myself more, or less, the daughter of Ann and Sid Wright. No matter what my behavior, I just *am*. However, I can express my love for them by *doing* things that show their likeness in my behavior. Being a daughter of God, the Father is the same. His pursuit of me by his act on the cross determines who I am. My showing his likeness in my behavior expresses my love for him.

My husband says that when I am undefinably blue or melancholy, I am longing for heaven—in a sense, mourning the lack of righteousness either in myself or the world around me. At that point I can choose to coddle myself and feel the hunger pangs, or I can pursue the goodness of God by *being* or *doing*, or both.

We will spiritually hunger and thirst until we arrive in heaven. The only way to satisfy that hunger and thirst is to eat and drink. Our experiences and emotions will sometimes attempt to fill us with spiritual "junk-food." But it won't satisfy. And we will be undefinably blue or melancholy, longing for heaven. Reminding ourselves of God's love for us and the righteousness we have because of Christ, and showing that in our behavior are the only things that will satisfy and fill us. If we will pursue God with total abandon, each day a new day, we will be satisfied.

DEVELOPING A PURE HEART

What is pure in heart (Matt. 5:8) other than the clay responding to the Potter's hand? We take our form from what we are pressed up against. In the natural world, the potter's hand warms the clay and it becomes pliable and responsive. And as the artist pushes and pulls the clay into form, it surrenders to the shape and will of the potter. In the spiritual sense, sometimes our hearts have become hard, and we have built such walls around them that we can't feel the hands of God on our lives. In those painfully quiet spiritual times, when we have loved our selves and our desires more than the Father's, we beg him for the patience to wait attentively for his leading in our lives once more. We will find that as pilgrims, the more we place ourselves in the hands of God, allowing him to melt the hardness of our hearts and passing from love of self to love of Christ, the more we will begin to reflect his image and will for our lives.

The psalmist pleads for his words—not just spoken but thought—to be pleasing to God (Ps. 19:4). While the scribes and Pharisees of Christ's era focused on the outward life with rules and regulations, Christ came and exposed the law as a surface understanding of loving God. The law brings with it temptation to live life collecting gold stars for our good behavior. But God desires to be in relationship with us from the inside out. Our interior love for him will affect our exterior actions, but that must not be confused with self-gain. Taking pride in our own goodness leads us back to self. A pure heart desires to find itself wholly holy in God.

Shallow cultural descriptions of perfection attempt to woo and pollute our hearts. Magazines with airbrush-perfect women tempt us to become engaged in a lifetime pursuit of the eighteen-year-old body and complexion. I feel so foolish when I discover that I know more about the perfect moisturizer and concealer than I do about engaging God in conversation. Obsessions with my own personal comfort and fulfillment become distractions when they are not second to my desire for God. It is Jesus, not myself, in whom all things are fitted and held together (Col. 1:17). Thomas à Kempis, who had a deep understanding of the pure love of God, said that "love of the created is deceptive and fickle: love of Jesus is faithful and steadfast."

Sometimes busying ourselves with exterior actions keeps us from dealing with the actual reality of spiritual surrender. We begin to pride ourselves in the things we are willing to do and do without and never get around to the surrender of the most important thing. Meister Eckhart cuts to the heart of the matter: "Plenty are willing to give up possessions, friends, honors, but it touches them too closely to disown themselves." A pride in exterior surrender avoids interior surrender.

A pure heart is unpolluted with desires of self, and instead desires to please the One beloved. The prayer that should sit on the door of our hearts is from W. H. Aitken: "Lord, take my lips and speak through them; take my mind, and think through it; take my heart, and set it on fire." And we will bear the image of God for having a pure heart and undivided affections.

FIXING OUR GAZE

The twelve-month period between fifteen and sixteen seems interminable. In northern Virginia, where I lived during this purgatory, you got a learner's permit to drive at fifteen and your official driver's license at age sixteen. During the learner's permit period, you could only drive a car with the company of a licensed driver. I remember imagining that I was soloing in our 1970 Cadillac, which was four inches wider than a metro bus. I would have the window down and rest my left arm there and drive the oversized land barge with my right hand.

I was allowed to take private driver's education classes. The public schools offered instruction, and everyone was required to take it before they could get a permanent license. But my birthday fell in such a way that I couldn't get into the class at school, so my generous parents paid for private lessons.

My driving instructor had his own very unique method of teaching. He did not use those strange two-steering-wheeled cars with all of the "WARNING! Student Driver on Board!" signs painted on them. We used normal cars, and eventually we used our own cars. He sat on the right-hand side of the car, and reached his feet across the floorboard to operate the peddles. Naturally, I found this strange, but I was the student, so I went with it. Eventually, you graduated to using the peddles yourself, but not until you had put in several weeks on steering alone.

Once the all-important steering was fairly under control, the peddles became yours. But that was not until around the tenth driving lesson out of twelve. You see, Mister Man's feeling was that if you could master steering, you could do anything. The hand-eye coordination involved in directing a moving vehicle takes careful study and lots of experience. It mostly takes up 90 percent of the skill qualification and relies on your ability to keep your eyes fixed on where you want to go. His philosophy was that you will drive toward what you look at. With so many things to look at, so much visual pollution, you have to discipline yourself to keep your eyes focused on where you are going, and just glance around once in a while to make yourself aware of where you are. If you are staring at the billboard advertising a getaway vacation, you will literally drive toward the billboard. Our bodies responsively follow where our eyes take us.

Most surely, our spiritual lives are parallel. What we fix our spiritual eyes on, we will aim our lives toward. The important thing here is to fix our eyes on something worth living our lives for.

Jesus had just done another superhuman act by feeding lunch to five thousand guests at an outdoor gathering with five loaves and two fishes. His culinary touch had netted leftovers, at that. After lunch, the disciples had gone on ahead of him in a boat to their next port of call (Matt. 14:22–31). Jesus stayed awhile and finished with the crowd, then took some solitude to pray. He was boatless, and when he was ready to catch up with the disciples, Jesus walked out on the water to their boat. He did this with no fanfare or spotlight, no grand announcement, but as if it were a normal form of transportation. It was a late and rough-tossed sea, and when the disciples finally looked up, they saw him walking toward them. Afraid he was a ghost, Peter, in authentic Galilean style, the living proof that testosterone existed before Monday Night Football, said, "If that's you, Lord, tell me to come to you on the water." Jesus responded with the same word he uses when you or I look into his eyes: "Come." In the next moment, Peter took a water-walk and believed the unbelievable. As long as he kept his gaze on Jesus, he walked.

Peter was walking, doing the impossible, until he became distracted by the waves and wind around him. When he took his gaze off Jesus, he started sinking fast. And Jesus, standing on an impossibility, *immediately* put his hand out and grabbed Peter's sinking hand. Just as Peter was safe after Jesus took his hand, when the God-hand holds our hands, we are safe.

As long as he kept his eyes focused on Jesus, Peter enjoyed a divine appointment of walking on water. When he trusted in his own senses, he sank. Do you trust your own senses more than the invitation from God to do something outside of your normal capabilities? If you keep your gaze on the face of Christ, you will live your life in reach of the hand of God.

Genesis 19:26 tells the story of a woman who couldn't stop staring at what was instead of looking forward into the face of "I Am." Even with God's promise of destroying her evil-thinking and evil-living town and his promise to rescue her and her family, in the middle of her deliverance, Mrs. Lot stiffened her neck and gave the glance of an unfaithful lover back to her home and her collection of things. We don't know exactly what made her look back, but whatever it was, it is clear that she willfully removed her gaze from God's promised future, trusting one last time in her own ways. She then became a silent salt figure staring at what was a poor imitation of treasure. For where our heart is, there is our treasure. What we fix our gaze on, we will pursue.

SIMPLE SUMMARY

When we recant our love of self and the world to love God, we commit to an undivided heart. But when we look back longingly at life lived on our terms, we become the harlot and flirt with death. The invitation to know and love God with our whole hearts is the generous invitation of rescue and redemption. How we can choose to look away is revealing of where the gaze of our spirits is focused.

God is the Irresistible Sovereign, in and through whom are all things (Rom. 11:36). Resisting him is like morning resisting the sunrise, or the shore rejecting the ocean's waves, or the moon refusing the light of the sun. Our foolishness and failings are part of our package, but they should not keep us from directing our spirits toward the love of Christ. Paul confessed his humanity, but strongly states his commitment to strain forward (Phil. 3:13–14). Focusing on the goal in our spiritual world can be no less.

Having a hunger and thirst for righteousness, developing a pure heart, and fixing our gaze on Christ are all characteristics of unreserved surrender. We make up our minds to life in God and are held there by the power of his Holy Spirit and the love of God for us. Nothing can separate us from that love. It is a flowing river that invades every inlet and corner of our spirits and flows over every jagged rock and unevenness.

Jesus tells two very short parables (Matt. 13:44–46) that succinctly describe how we are to desire Christ in our lives. In one, a person comes upon a treasure in a field and sells everything to put together the capital to buy the field so that he can get the treasure in it. In the second, a wise pearl merchant finds the ideal pearl he had been searching for and sells everything he has to buy it. One comes upon the treasure by accident, and one comes upon it by deliberate search, but each knows that everything else pales in comparison to the treasure when they find it.

Do I really, *really* live there? Do I desire to be wholly holy his? Do I recognize the real Treasure, or am I a silent salt woman because I've betrayed the Beloved with the things and pursuits of self?

When we are being swallowed by the busyness of life, when the trivial is disguised as essential, when we are drowning in worry and anxiety about the future, we have lost our focus. If we are to refocus on the goal of loving God with our whole hearts, we have to empty ourselves of self, and in that emptiness, encounter the muchness of God.

12

SUMMARY OF
PART III

"Smell is a potent wizard that transports us across thousands of miles and all the years we have lived," said Helen Keller, who was keenly aware of the mysterious, unseeable thing called fragrance. Scents are strong, invisible name tags. The women in my mother's office know when she is in without ever seeing her because they can smell her perfume as it lingers in the hallway. When we are apart, I like to sleep in one of Jim's shirts because they smell like him. And if I close my eyes, I can smell Old Spice from my dad kissing me good morning when he woke me up every day in high school.

Jim and I traveled to France to celebrate our twentieth anniversary and visited the Fragonard perfumerie. They explained to us that many years ago, in an effort to boost the leather glove trade by scenting them, the French invented a method of extracting scent from flowers. It became so popular that it outlasted the glove market and became its own industry.

The earliest method was *enfleurage*, a romantic technique based on the principle that some animal fats have a strong natural attraction for aromas. It is like when you leave butter uncovered in the refrigerator, and it takes on the smells around it. So they smeared fat onto sheets of glass in wooden frames then sandwiched flowers between the trays and changed out for fresh ones when they faded. Eventually, the fat became saturated with the aroma and was beaten with alcohol in mechanical churns for a week. The fragrance transferred to the alcohol and was aged like wine for up to a year.

Now, a more efficient method known as distillation is used to extract the aroma from flowers. In an alembic, a sealed stainless steel apparatus, flowers and five times their weight in water are combined and brought to a boil. The steam absorbs the aromatic particles and passes through chilled water in the coil where the essence condenses. The condensed mixture of essential oil and water drips into the "essencier," where they are naturally separated by their differing weights. Two hundred pounds of lavender flowers are necessary to create one pound of essence. And more than three thousand pounds of roses are required for one pound of a rose scent.

So once the tedious process of distilling is complete, the job of creating a perfume is put to the "noses." These are a handful of gifted craftsmen and women who can distinguish some six thousand different fragrances. The "nose" blends fragrances referred to as the "key note," which is the most obvious scent, the "core note" or character scent, and the "basic note," which holds it all together. These olfactory wonders mix fruity, tart, woody, flowery, or sensual smells to create the resulting perfumes. The product of their labors scent necks and wrists all over the world.

The meticulous process of perfume making involves patience, diligence, and a master's touch. The result benefits the wearer and those around them, and the master is pleased with the creation.

The mysterious invisible world of the spirit is the same. It is at times tedious and confining as the Master turns the heat up in our lives and then takes the essence of our experience and discipline and delicately combines them with his Holy Spirit, who holds it all together, to create a spiritual life within us. And people will know and identify us by the fragrance of our spirits. Paul says in 2 Corinthians 2:14–15 that God spreads the fragrance of the knowledge of him everywhere through us. The same as I went to school smelling like Old Spice for my dad having hugged me, we bear the smell of Christ for having spent time in his presence. And it becomes an invisible name tag.

This identifying scent is distilled in us when we are in right relationship with God and sin isn't cluttering the path. It is produced from the habits of holiness in our everyday lives. And it is strongest when we have been in the Presence. Tolstoy said God is the One who brings all things together that are splintered, scattered, and spreading away from the center. When he brings all things together in our spiritual lives, we are a sweet aroma, and a fragrance of Christ.

WORKING IT OUT

1. Do you recognize truth as being objective and determined by God? Are there areas of life where you live like it is subjective and up to the individual? Choose to live by the plumb line.

2. I have been made clean and have received God's forgiveness. (Answer "yes" or "no.")

3. If the answer to number 2 was "no," you must be made clean by confessing your sins, cleaning out the spiritual closet, mourning your sin, and receiving forgiveness. You will find yourself here repeatedly in your spiritual life. In the same way as you can't clean out your clothes closet once and expect it to stay that way forever, you need to readdress your spiritual closet often.

4. Have you committed to being a pilgrim instead of a tourist? Have you begun to hold the ocean one handful at a time?

5. A commitment to Habits of Holiness will help to keep you in the presence of God, and help you know him one day at a time.

   - *Meditation.* Commit to a time of still and deep. Think on the nature of Christ and his work in you. Start with a short time, maybe when you wake up, or when you got to bed. Build from there.

   - *Prayer.* Consider purchasing a book of prayers to help in those dry times. Do you have a "place" to pray? If you made one, would it help facilitate a time to pray? Pray your heart, and listen.

   - *Fasting.* Pray about what kind of fast to take—lunch, a whole day, or longer. Be prepared to be unmasked and to bloom.

   - *The Eucharist.* Whatever form you use, remember the sacrifice of Christ for your salvation. He came to invade your everyday life. Do you live that way?

- *Worship.* Do you delight in God? Music, nature, corporate worship, prayer, and the other habits of holiness are ways to delight in him.
6. Are you planting vital seeds in your spiritual life? What is growing?
7. Are you zigzagging through the journey, or do you have your focus on the infinite reference point?
8. To focus on being wholly his, ask the Holy Spirit to:
   - build a hunger and thirst for righteousness. What do you need to empty yourself of to make room for that hunger and thirst?
   - drive you to develop a pure heart. What is your heart polluted with? Are your affections divided?
   - give you faith to fix your gaze. What are you looking at in your life? Are you trusting yourself and your senses, or are you responding to the invitation to walk on water?
9. Take time to sit still in the middle of the frantic pace of life, focus on the interior life, and wait for him to meet you there.

Prayer: Oh God, help me simplify in spirit. I must be made clean from my sins and agree with you that they are wrong. Let your forgiveness wash over me. By your Spirit, establish habits of holiness in me to keep me in your presence. Help me to keep my eyes on you, that I could walk a supernatural walk on water. May I bear the scent of your Son that others may know your life. I want to be so wholly yours that I am holy, yours.

SPIRIT: AT A GLANCE

- Be supernaturally laundered.
- Reduce the clutter. Get rid of the sin in your life. Identify the plumb line, make a good confession, and then receive forgiveness.
- Persevere in the everyday. Become a pilgrim and establish habits of holiness: meditation, prayer, fasting, the Eucharist, and worship.
- Focus on the goal. Have a heart wholly after God. Hunger and thirst for righteousness, pursue a pure heart, and fix your gaze on the infinite reference point.

CONCLUSION:
SIMPLY SAID

My cousin and her family always had all the good stuff. They had one of those little Coke machines with the little bitty glasses. It was like having your own soda fountain. She had an Easy-Bake Oven, Thumbelina doll, and breasts before I did. They had a dune buggy that we all rode around in with my preteen cousin driving, and, miraculously, we all survived. They had a swimming pool, motorcycles, Ping Pong table, pool table, horses, and a riding lawn mower over the course of my childhood.

So when she came to visit me at our rented house in Arlington, Virginia, I really had to rack my brain to come up with something exotic and exciting for our summer entertainment. I didn't have the bells and whistles in my toy arsenal, but I was never lacking for imagination. And, frankly, anything we did, as long as we did it together, was a fun and memorable adventure.

It took me a good twenty minutes to rinse out the rubber thirty-gallon trash cans that were stored in our garage. Fortunately, trash pick-up had been two days before. But the real waiting with baited breath began as we placed the hose into one of the garbage cans and waited for it to fill up. In ever-increasing excitement, we waited for the other one to fill up before we finally crawled into them. Bottoms plunged into the cool, refreshing water, legs and arms hanging out over the edge, we made something out of nothing, learned contentment, and made a memory that turns up the edges of my mouth even now.

Simplicity is not a call to a monastic life of austerity and doing without, but a call to contentment, which is the core of the abundant life. Simplifying our body, soul, and spirit by reducing the clutter, persevering in the everyday, and focusing on the goal frees us to discover contentment and helps us see something in nothing.

As we examined specific ways to simplify our lives, you may have become overwhelmed. The suggestions may make you feel bogged down as you begin to implement them at first, but don't give up. It is the matter of investing now that will give you the return of peace, definition, and wholeness in the long run. We are not looking for perfection in the unattainable sense, but wholeness in the holy sense. Eugene Peterson's *The Message* paraphrases the words of 1 Thessalonians 5:23 beautifully: "May God himself, the God who makes everything holy and whole, make you holy and whole, put you together—spirit, soul, and body—and keep you fit for the coming of our Master, Jesus Christ."

So fearlessly reduce, persevere and focus, my friend. Cut away the things that don't look like his image and net the beautiful benefits of simplicity by having a life patterned after God. And as you begin to speak order into your life, you will reflect the image of God, who spoke order into the universe in the very beginning.

ENDNOTES

CHAPTER 1

1. Thomas Merton, *"No Man Is an Island"* (New York: Harcourt and Brace), p. 100.

CHAPTER 2

1. The Positive Press, http://www.positivepress.com
2. The Science About Ants, http://members.aol.com/dinarda/ant/index.htm

CHAPTER 3

1. Stephen Covey, *The 7 Habits of Highly Effective People* (New York: Simon & Schuster, 1989).
2. Charles Hummel, *Tyranny of the Urgent* (Downers Grove, Ill.: InterVarsity Press, 1971).

CHAPTER 5

1. Dietrich Bonhoeffer, *The Cost of Discipleship.*
2. Unhealthy relationships. People who are manipulators, monopolizers, users, competers, takers, compulsively needy, liars, or abusers, are not great candidates for thriving healthy relationships. In some extreme cases, the synthesis for an unhealthy relationship is to part company. If a person won't be reasoned with, the only choice you have is to walk away. In the story of the prodigal son, the father allowed the son to leave and did not pursue him. It was only when the son came to his senses and returned home and repented that fellowship was restored. It took both parties, one repenting and one offering forgiveness.

CHAPTER 6

1. Andrew Murray, *With Christ in the School of Prayer* (Kansas City, Mo.: Beacon Hill Press).
2. Frederick Buechner, *Godric* (San Francisco: HarperCollins, 1980).
3. A year set aside in the Old Testament when all debts were canceled and all land that had been sold was returned (see Lev. 25).

CHAPTER 7

1. Stephen R. Covey, *The 7 Habits of Highly Effective People.*
2. Epitaphs found online at:
   http://www.best.com/~gazissax/silence/epitaphs/index.html.
3. Greek, *makarios,* meaning "unmovable, unassailable happiness."
4. Laurie Beth Jones, *The Path* (New York: Hyperion, 1996).
5. Dorothy Sayers, *The Whimsical Christian* , pp. 86 and 87.

PART III: SPIRIT

1. C. S. Lewis, *The Lion, the Witch, and the Wardrobe* (New York: Collier/Macmillan, 1970). This book describes the "Christ" character, Aslan, as not safe, but good.
2. Eugene Peterson, *A Long Obedience in the Same Direction* (Downers Grove, Ill.: InterVarsity Press, 1980).

CHAPTER 9

1. Josh McDowell and Bob Hostetler, *Right from Wrong* (Dallas: Word, 1994).
2. Richard J. Foster, *Celebration of Discipline* (New York: Harper & Row, 1978, 1988).
3. Eugene Peterson, *Take and Read* (Grand Rapids: Eerdmans, 1996).
4. http://emporium.turnpike.net/C/cs/breakpt.htm. *It's Not Sin, It's an Adaptation: Natural Evil* (Prison Fellowship, BreakPoint radio series, 1993).
5. John R. W. Stott, *The Message of the Sermon on the Mount* (Downers Grove, Ill.: InterVarsity Press, 1978).
6. William Barclay, *The Gospel of Matthew, Volume 1,* revised edition (Philadelphia, Penn.: Westminster Press, 1975).
7. *Bits & Pieces,* October 15, 1992, p. 13.
8. C.S. Lewis Quote

CHAPTER 10

1. François Fenelon, *Christian Perfection* (Minneapolis, Minn.: Bethany House Publishers, 1975).
2. Evelyn Underhill, *Mystics of the Church* (Morehouse Publishing).
3. Thomas Merton, *Thoughts in Solitude* (New York: Farrar, Straus and Giroux).
4. While Paul doesn't mention fasting in this passage, he is speaking of the greater analogy of how the spiritual life blossoms even though the outer life, the flesh, may be wasting away.
5. Two Old Testament examples are Moses on Mount Sinai when he received the Ten Commandments from the Lord (Exod. 34:28) and Daniel, who fasted for three weeks to understand a vision he was given (Dan. 10:3).
6. Other New Testament references are in Mark 9:21–29 where fasting accompanied prayer in the casting out of spirits, and in Acts 14:23 where Paul and Barnabas fasted when they committed the new elders to the Lord, and Acts 13 where the Lord first commissioned Saul and Barnabas.
7. Rainer Maria Rilke, *Letters to a Young Poet* (W. W. Norton & Co., 1934).
8. John Piper, *Desiring God* (Portland, Oreg.: Multnomah Press, 1986).

CHAPTER 11

1. William Barclay, *The Gospel of Matthew, Volume 1* (Philadelphia, Penn.: Westminster Press, 1975).

ABOUT THE AUTHOR

Kim Thomas is a writer, speaker, painter, and performer. As the modern pop duo Say-So, Kim and her husband Jim have recorded two CDs for the Organic Records/Pamplin Music label—*Say-So* and their recent release, *Still Waters*. Kim and Jim travel, speak, and perform at conferences and retreats. The couple recently celebrated twenty years of marriage. They make their home in Nashville with their two dogs, Rose and Violet.

For booking information, E-mail Kim at

SaySofans@aol.com

or write to her at P.O. Box 121954, Nashville, TN 37212.